111 Places in the Lake District That You Shouldn't Miss

111

emons:

To Andy. May there be exciting trips, always.

© Emons Verlag GmbH
Photographs by Solange Berchemin, except Blackwell Arts: ch. 14;
Wordsworth Trust: ch. 38; shutterstock.com/Philip Downie: ch. 55;
Stacey MacNaught: ch. 72; Graham Wynne: ch. 79;
John Shortland (www.jdshortlandwriter.com): ch. 104
© Cover motif: shutterstock.com/RuudMorijnPhoto
Layout: Eva Kraskes, based on a design
by Lübbeke | Naumann | Thoben
Edited by Alison Lester
Maps: altancicek.design, www.altancicek.de
Basic cartographical information from Openstreetmap,
© OpenStreetMap-Mitwirkende, ODbL
Printing and binding: Grafisches Centrum Cuno, Calbe
Printed in Germany 2024
ISBN 978-3-7408-2404-4
First edition 2019
Revised fourth edition, October 2024

Guidebooks for Locals & Experienced Travellers
Join us in uncovering new places around the world at
www.111places.com

Foreword

The Lake District claims some of England's best-loved destinations and is a UNESCO World Heritage site on a par with the Great Barrier Reef Park and the Galápagos Islands. Each year, over 20 million visitors come to enjoy the magnificent fells glimmering with golden light and the tarns reflecting their beauty.

Superlative-seekers will find the deepest, the highest, the most Instagrammed places – though I tried to avoid the wettest. When locations were well known, I made sure to peek into their inmost corners. Readers will travel perched on the platform of the much-loved La'al Ratty and stroll to the delicately sculpted National Trust birthday stone. They will learn how the worldwide Marmalade Competition was born out of a will to help farmers during the foot-and-mouth epidemic, how paint-makers saved a disused iron ore mine, and where to find the tallest Viking cross. Sure, the Romantic poets, Beatrix Potter and Ruskin's haunts are included but so are the little-known Laurel & Hardy Museum and the first woman architect's moving tribute to her loved ones.

The region is also fantastic to visit thanks to the Cumbrians who live and work here. Loving their environs so much, they volunteered their own stories and those of their ancestors. The curators, ex-miners, brewers and many others I met unknowingly put a pin on the map and made this book *their* book. They provided the warmth necessary to fuel yet another foray, whatever the weather, from the Kadampa Buddhist temple in Ulverston to the 'Cracker Packers' statue in Carlisle.

This guide is arranged in alphabetical order by towns, including sites in easy reach of those places, so that these groups of chapters constitute an itinerary. May visiting them delight you as much as they did me. This area of north-west England may be compact, but like its tarns it mirrors and beautifies our quest for secret places to love.

111 Places

1__Jenkin's Crag

Hug the tallest trees in England

This attractive, energic walk will call on all your senses. For a convenient start head to Waterhead at the northern end of Lake Windermere. The crag offers an outlook over the lake and the central peaks of the Langdales with the unmissable shape of the Old Man of Coniston. It is easy to find, and clearly signposted all the way. Like all walks, it can be made as short or as long as you wish, with the option to continue on to Troutbeck. It may not seem very promising at first as it climbs steeply through an alleyway backing houses. But the path soon reaches an open field where you can pick up the trail into the ancient woodland of Skelghyll Wood via a four-step stile. In the spring the woodland is filled with the pungent aroma of wild garlic whilst a carpet of bluebells covers the ground. At any other time a damp-moss smell creates a special atmosphere.

Skelghyll Wood is renowned for its monumental trees. You'll find one of the tallest grand fir trees in England, which stood at 57.8 metres at the last measure in 2012. Understandably, Lake District rangers are not sent too often to the top to measure its progress. The tallest grand fir in the world is near Vancouver, Canada. At 75.29 metres it is comparable in height to the giant sequoias in California. This walk links nicely with the Ambleside Champion Tree Trail, a 45-minute circular route through the woods, which is signposted from the car park. Just follow the tree symbols. On the way back, you may have just enough energy for a detour to the National Trust's pretty Stagshaw Garden, which can be found via a gate on the opposite side of the small car park. It includes a lovely collection of plants including rhododendrons, azaleas and camellias. It is also your opportunity to indulge in an ice cream or a cream cake. After all, you've just walked enough to burn the calories.

Address Start at Waterhead car park, Borrans Road, Ambleside, LA22 0ES | Getting there South of Ambleside town centre, opposite the Windermere Cruise launch site, park in the pay-and-display car park. Walk back onto Borrans Road, turn left towards the Waterhead Hotel, cross (carefully) over A 591. A sign to Jenkins Crag is directly opposite. | Access Year-round; parts can be muddy | Tip The nearby Stock Ghyll Force is another local walk through the woods, and leads to a waterfall (Ambleside, LA22 0QT).

2 Low Wood Bay Sculptures

Local fauna in 3D

Cumbria is certainly not short of sculpture trails, nor is there a lack of talented artists working in the area. As often, the adverse weather conditions can be an impediment; after a while, sculptures are so weather-worn that they lose definition. As you may expect, some resist better than others, a good few are now difficult to identify. Learning from past mistakes the new trails should last for longer.

Low Wood Bay Sculpture Trail was commissioned by the Low Wood Bay Resort & Spa, and created by local artist and stone mason Shawn Williamson, who has been working as a sculptor for a quarter of a century and is best known for his big stone sculptures such as his 19-ton Herdwick ram. In 1985, he was pupil and assistant to the internationally known Lakeland artist Josefina de Vasconcellos (see ch. 44), who had herself been mentored by no less than Rodin, the French master. For the duration of the project, Williamson became the artist in residence at the resort.

He worked with 12 reclaimed boulders chosen from among the material unearthed during the excavations undertaken during the resort's major renovations. The trail theme turns exclusively around the local fauna, and the result is a trail of animals on the Ambleside shore of Lake Windermere.

Lakeland has extraordinary wildlife and this type of project also has an educational purpose. The boulders are here to show tourists and the local public the type of creatures that can be found in the surrounding countryside and in the lake. This is a nice walk to do with young children. Start by the jetty, opposite the resort, with the fish boulder. Continue along the path and very soon you'll see the otter and other animal stones. There is one stone – an odd man out – that doesn't represent local fauna on this trail. It is a 3D portrait of Michael Berry, former owner of the resort, with his dog.

Address Ambleside Road, near Ambleside, Windermere, LA23 1LP | Getting there The sculptures are mostly dotted along the shoreline. The easiest way to see them is to park in the ticketed car park opposite the resort. Low Wood Bay is on A 591 between Ambleside and Windermere; it is a brisk 30-minute walk from the centre of Ambleside; bus 555 stops near the resort. | Access Year-round | Tip Low Wood Bay is located next to the jetties where the annual Great North Swim is launched. The Great North is a major open-water swim taking place over three days with around 10,000 participants (www.greatrun.org/great-swim).

3_ Schwitters at the Armitt
Dada in Cumbria

The Armitt is a fascinating museum, gallery and library. Since it is located in the heart of the Lake District, in the town of Ambleside, it would be natural for visitors to expect only works by local artists. For that reason, several rooms devoted to the German Dadaist Kurt Schwitters come as a surprise. In fact, the permanent collection here houses the largest number of works by this artist, one of the 20th-century greats.

Kurt Schwitters was best known for his collages, harbingers of pop art. Born in Hanover in 1887, in his early years Schwitters experimented with several genres and media: Cubism, Expressionism, Dadaism, Constructivism to name but a few. In 1937, he fled Nazi Germany, narrowly escaping arrest by the Gestapo. On hearing about the concentration camps, Schwitters renounced his German nationality. From then on, he refused to speak a word of German and fled first to Norway, then to Great Britain where he was interned for over a year. On release, with his health declining, he moved to rural Cumbria. Ambleside must have looked like a strange and rustic town to the artist, but it inspired simultaneously some of his most conventional and his most avant-garde works. In the hope of making a living whilst in Ambleside, he painted portraits, flowers and landscapes in a traditional manner to appeal to the tourists and the wealthy locals. Thirty of his paintings and pencil drawings can be seen at the Armitt Museum, including a striking 1945 painting of the Bridge House.

Schwitters' most influential work was his Merz Barns, installations in barns containing 3D abstract collages made out of all sorts of discarded and broken items. There is very little left of his Lake District barn, in Elterwater, unfinished at his death in 1948, but the Armitt Museum collection includes one of his collages called *Wood on Wood*.

Address Rydal Road, Ambleside, LA22 9BL | **Getting there** From the south, follow A 591, pass the Bridge House, cross the mini-roundabout, take the first right turn. From the north, follow A 591 past Green Bank Road, take the left turn just before the mini-roundabout. Bus 555 and 599 will take you to Ambleside, Keswick or Lancaster. The pay-and-display car park is opposite the museum. | **Hours** Tue – Sat 10.30am – 4.30pm | **Tip** Schwitters is buried in St Mary's Church in Ambleside. His grave is marked with one of his sculptures, *Die Herbstzeilose*.

4_ The Knoll

Home to the first woman journalist

Harriet Martineau was born in 1802, the sixth child of a wealthy Unitarian manufacturer. Described as a 'Victorian superstar', she quickly established a wide circle of influential friends including George Eliot, Charlotte Brontë, Dickens, Nightingale and the Wordsworths. Erasmus Darwin, Charles' brother, was one of her admirers. But she was no socialite; she had a powerful intellect and a gift for describing clearly what she observed. She pursued a unique career in journalism and was the first woman sociologist.

The Knoll in Ambleside was her home from 1844 until her death in 1876. The tall, two-storey, square house of stone rubble with a slate roof, and beautiful views towards Loughrigg (see ch. 40), was built to her own design. Today it's a private home. When she lived here, Harriett threw regular parties during which she asked her guests to plant two trees. As a result, the garden is now lush.

The Martineau family were of French Huguenot stock, free-thinking immigrants who fled the religious persecutions of 17th-century France. Harriet's father, Thomas, is great-great-great-great-great-grandfather to Catherine, Duchess of Cambridge (Kate Middleton). Harriet herself had very little time for the monarchy. She was invited to Queen Victoria's coronation, and found nothing much more to report on than the sandwiches.

Profoundly deaf from her teenage years, she explained in her biography the difficulties she faced and the determination she needed to be accepted as a socio-political writer in a world of men. Her atheism didn't help either. She went to America where she identified with the anti-slavery cause. She wrote more than 50 books, a wide range of articles – over 1,500 in the *Daily News* alone. Each was keenly awaited by the public and the political class alike. Inspired by Lakeland she also produced a guidebook for the budding tourist crowd.

Address 1 The Knoll, Rydal Road, Ambleside, LA22 9AY | **Getting there** The Knoll can only be seen from a distance. It sits off A 591, on the left when heading towards Grasmere, past Rydal Road Car Park and Stoney Lane. Park in one of the public car parks, walk along A 591, turn into Stoney Lane and take the public footpath at the end. | **Access** Private property, but always visible | **Tip** Another Ambleside house to view is the bridge house over Stock Ghyll Beck, one of the most photographed scenes in the Lakes, and an interesting place to visit.

5 Armathwaite Signal Box

Colourfully obsolete

The Settle – Carlisle line, completed by the Midland Railway Company in 1876, had a transformative impact over the North of England. One of the major changes was the increase in the number of tourists in beauty spots.

Due to its geographical position amidst the epic landscapes of Cumbria and North Yorkshire, the line is a feat of engineering. Over 72 miles of tracks and 380 bridges were built, including 21 viaducts, 14 tunnels and 1 aqueduct. Those are the predominant features but others too were essential for the smooth running of operations. Signal boxes, most now made obsolete by the advance of technology, were vital to ensure that trains didn't collide. Trains don't manoeuvre around obstacles, train drivers need guidance. At first, this was the job of the pointmen with their individual levers and semaphore signals, but when the traffic got too heavy, the levers were brought together under one roof.

The signal box at Armathwaite Station was brought into service on 16 July, 1899 and closed in 1983. Volunteer members of Friends of the Settle – Carlisle Line restored the building in 1992. The previous one had suffered fire damage. Sitting pretty, a little way away from the platform, the rebuilt wooden construction with its tiled roof is now a small museum. It contains the original 16-lever frame and interesting exhibits related to the history of the place and of the famous line. Many instruments to control the box have been returned to their original position. It is open for accompanied tours most Sundays and on request. The building's striking colours, bright yellow and brown, were the original colours of the Midland Railway Company. Picking the correct shade might have been a problem as original colour photographs were rare and often misleading. The only thing we know is that pre-nationalisation, railways were a colourful affair.

Address Armathwaite Station, CA4 9PW, +44 (0)7759 593224, www.foscl.org.uk/scrca/ structure-summary/298220, john.johnson@settle-carlisle.com | Getting there By car, take A6 from Carlisle or Penrith and look out for sign to Armathwaite. Parking spaces are beside the entrance to the northbound platform. The signal box is located beyond the end of the southbound platform. No foot-crossing allowed, so walk down the country lane on the north side, then up a steep path to the southbound platform. By train, take Northern Rail to Armathwaite. | Hours Sun 10am–5pm, 4pm in winter. Contact station if you plan to visit outside opening hours. | Tip Railway-themed walks are organised by Friends of the Settle–Carlisle Line (www.foscl.org.uk/guided-walks/armathwaite-signal-box-visit-railway-walk).

6 __ Sarah Losh's Legacy
Italia in Cumbria

Thanks to Sarah Losh's creative genius, Wreay is a must-see destination for any visitor in Cumbria. Born in 1785 into a prominent local family, Sarah, in her early thirties, accompanied her sister Katharine, whom she loved dearly, on a grand tour of France, Germany and Italy. Once there, she drew, watched, learned and came back full of a newly found knowledge. The painter and poet Dante Gabriel Rosetti wrote about her in a letter, saying, 'She must have been really a great genius, and should be better known.'

Sarah created St Mary's Church in memory of her sister Katharine who died young. She designed it, worked on it and paid for it. This was not the first building she designed and all of her work is truly beautiful. There had been a church at Wreay for a very long time but in 1840, the old chapel was falling apart. Sarah donated the funds for a new one on the condition that she 'should be left unrestricted as to the mode of building it'.

She based its architecture on the ancient Roman basilicas used by early Christians. Wherever you look, you'll see a symbolic element, most of which refer to death and rebirth, and their stylisation prefigures that of the Arts and Crafts Movement, which happened 50 years later. The arrows on the door panels and embedded in the wall refer to death. They recall her friend Major William Thain who was killed by an arrow when his battalion was ambushed retreating from Afghanistan. The church is alive with creatures: bats evoking darkness, cockerel for light. Look carefully, there is a dragon acting as a chimney. Nature is everywhere – lotuses on candlesticks; pinecones, symbols of regeneration and inner enlightenment; gargoyles, which Sarah called 'emblematic monsters'. St Mary's is not her only creation. Sarah Losh's design legacy also includes three wells, two schools, several houses, a mausoleum, to name only a few.

Address St Mary's Church, Wreay, CA4 0RJ, +44 (0)1228 710215, www.stmaryswreay.org | **Getting there** Wreay is 5.4 miles south of Carlisle, 3 miles from J 42 of M 6. The church is near the Plough Inn, on-street parking is available in front of the church. Stagecoach bus 104 (Penrith – Carlisle) stops in front of the church on demand. | **Hours** Daily 10am – 4pm, please respect the services | **Tip** In the Chapel of Rest, Sarah's first building, there is the Sarah Losh Heritage Centre. Friends of St Mary's Church have put together a very informative leaflet and organise walks exploring Sarah Losh's life and work. Open during the same hours as the church.

7 Arnside

Fish, chips and sunsets

Once a quiet fishing village, Arnside, situated on the Cumbria-Lancashire border, found its place as the gateway to the Lake District, though it still remains an unspoiled holiday destination. Transport developments played a large role in its growth. In the 19th century, the construction of a 500-metre-long railway viaduct across the River Kent contributed to the good fortune of the local economy and without any doubt changed the scenery. But it is the pleasure boats sailing from Morecambe and Fleetwood that contributed most to the tourist boom. Ships dropped affluent passengers ashore, for them to enjoy the famous Promenade walks and sample the local delicacies: salmon and potted shrimps. Two centuries later, the Promenade pubs, cafés and shops are still a pull for people on vacation who come to admire the spectacular sunsets and enjoy the famous Arnside fish and chips.

Sunsets across Morecambe Bay are certainly a technicolour spectacle. Some even say that they are the best displays in the world, and are free of the usual crowds which often spoil such sights. Drivers, blinking in the evening sun, tend to zoom along the A6 road to reach the south lakes quickly, leaving Arnside and Silverdale, its twin village, behind, taking no notice of their Outstanding Natural Beauty status.

The sunset experience is not complete without a visit to the Arnside Chip Shop and the Big Chip Café located at the north end of the Promenade. Run by David Miller and his sons, the shop with its bow-window and backwards clock deserves its reputation. Best seasonal potatoes, of course, and meaty fish in light crispy batter straight from the fryer make for an excellent meal or takeaway. It's not only word-of-mouth spreading the message, it's technology too. This is one of the few fish and chip shops in the country equipped with a live webcam feed.

Address The Arnside Chip Shop and the Big Chip Café, 1 The Promenade, Arnside, LA5 0HF, +44 (0)1524 761874, www.arnsidechipshop.co.uk, arnsidechipshop@gmail.com | **Getting there** By car via M6 exit at J35; from A6 it is between Milnthorpe and Carnforth. Arnside station is a stop on the Lancaster to Carlisle and the Barrow-in-Furness to Preston lines. Stagecoach bus 551, 552 from Kendal and 555 from Lancaster via Carnforth, or 99 from The Promenade to Kendal and Kirkby Lonsdale. | **Hours** Tue–Thu 11.30am–1.45pm & 4.30–7:30pm, Fri 11.30am–2pm & 4.30–8pm, Sat 11.30am–8pm, Sun noon–7.30pm or earlier in the winter | **Tip** A bore is a rare and impressive tidal phenomenon, and can come down the River Kent as fast as a galloping horse, with high waves. A siren is sounded twice before a bore. Canoeists come from miles around to take advantage of the incoming water.

8 Lakeland Motor Museum

Vroom, vroom

Lakeland Motor Museum is situated in gorgeous purpose-built buildings by the River Leven at Backbarrow, near Newby. The museum moved from the stables at Holker Hall (see ch. 19) to the current site in 2010. The museum, occupying as it does the former 'Dolly Blue' packing-shed plot, became an instantaneous landmark. The ultramarine pigment used in laundry powder (among other things) was a dominant industry in the area, and the blue museum buildings make a strong reference to the recent industrial past of Leven Valley.

Enter, follow the timeline and walk down memory lane, in order to come away with a better understanding of the evolution of car manufacturing. Feast your eyes on classic cars, motorbikes and the largest collection of automobilia: petrol pumps, globes, car mascots and enamel advertising signs. In fact, it was the founder's keen interest in advertising that gave rise to this 30,000-strong collection.

The collection is half-owned, half-borrowed, and the museum changes its display often to keep visitors interested. You don't have to be a petrol-head to love this collection, as there is something for everyone. The oldest exhibit is an 1899 tricycle, found in 1937 in a scrapyard, and surviving in its highly original state to this day. Car safety is a feature too, from vintage cars without front brakes or windscreen to 1959 models which were the first to be fitted with seat belts. It's difficult to know which vehicle stands out most. It could be the smallest car in the world, the 1964 Peep P50; or the fastest road-going car ever produced, the 2000 TVR Cerbera Speed 12; or even your own childhood car. There is something for everyone and every little bit of space is used. Housed in its own unique building there is an exhibition dedicated to the Campbells, Sir Malcolm and his son Donald, who set land and water speed records (see ch. 29). There also is a café with views of the river.

Address Old Blue Mill, Backbarrow, Ulverston, LA12 8TA, +44 (0)1539 530400, www.lakelandmotormuseum.co.uk | Getting there The museum is adjacent to A590 between Newby Bridge and Haverthwaite, with free parking on site; the Stagecoach X6 stops opposite | Hours Daily 10am–6pm | Tip Combine a visit to the museum with a boat trip on Lake Windermere. The combined museum and boat tickets represent a good saving. A minibus is available to take visitors from the boat landing to the museum.

9 ___ Stott Park Bobbin Mill

'Happy hour' it's not

South of Lake Windermere, you'll find a 19th-century time capsule. In the 1830s, when tourism was in its infancy, the region relied on industries that took advantage of the environment. Stream water provided power, and coppiced woodland offered the raw material for the local mills, an important part of the national economy. Stott Park Bobbin Mill was founded in 1835, one of 40 such mills in the area serving the growing textile industry and the infamous cotton mills of Manchester, which required millions of bobbins.

Turning wood into bobbins was a dangerous, fast-paced, profit-hungry business. Some bobbins were rather large while others, known as 'caps', were very small. Caps were required for the delicate work of the silk 'throwsters', or spinners. To bore them, workers had to be very skilled and extremely vigilant, otherwise they could easily lose their fingers. Horrific accidents involving loss of limbs in fast-moving leather belts were not uncommon. Luckily, no deaths were recorded at this mill. Boys as young as 8 years old were employed until 1878, when a law regulating child labour was passed and the minimum age was raised to 11.

A 45-minute guided tour of the mill is a unique opportunity to understand the manufacturing process and the working conditions of Lakeland dwellers during the Industrial Revolution. The mill buildings have been faithfully restored and the machines repaired. Demonstrations make the process all the more vivid to understand what happened from the moment the coppiced wood was stripped of its bark to the final process.

Gluing and staining were done by one worker during the last hour of the working week. This was referred to as 'happy hour' on account of the chemical inhaled. When the mill closed in 1971, its production had diversified one last time: it had been able to take advantage of the yo-yo craze.

Address Colton Hill, Ulverston, LA12 8AX, +44 (0)1539 531087, www.english-heritage.org.uk/visit/places/stott-park-bobbin-mill | **Getting there** By car, located 1.5 miles north of Newby Bridge, off A 590; by train, Grange-over-Sands station is 8 miles away; by boat, Windermere Lake Cruises from Ambleside or Bowness to Lakeside, then a three-quarter-mile walk; bus 538 (Thu only) passes the site, or take X32 to Newby Bridge (summer only) | **Hours** Sept–Nov, Wed–Sun 10am–5pm; visit the website for other times during the yearIf you are interested in more of the area's industrial past, contact Cumbria Industrial History Society (www. cumbria-industries.org.uk). | **Tip** If you are interested in more of the area's industrial past, contact Cumbria Industrial History Society (www. cumbria-industries.org.uk).

10 Bassenthwaite Lake

Big bird, little fish, and skulduggery

Bassenthwaite Lake gently shimmers under the mighty Skiddaw, one of England's highest mountains. It's the most northerly large body of water in Lakeland, and the only one with 'lake' in its name. Four miles long and only three-quarters of a mile wide, its shape resembles a finger, its waters are very shallow. But don't expect its shores to be bustling with people. Most of the shoreline is privately owned, and only members of the Sailing Club can launch their boats on the water.

Unless you've booked a stay in one of the lakeshore hotels or villas, the closest you will get to the lake is by stopping at one of the A 66 lay-bys or at the lake viewing point, on the west shore. However, this overall relatively quiet atmosphere doesn't mean that the area lacks attractions. At the northern end, there is Dubwath Silver Meadows Nature Reserve, which is considered as the first ever wetland nature reserve of high importance for birds nesting in England. Bassenthwaite Lake attracts over 80 species of bird, including wild ospreys (see ch. 60), all here for rich pickings. It is also one of only two places in Britain where the endangered vendace fish can be found.

Mire House, opposite Dodd Wood car park, provides the locality with a bookish attraction. The Spedding family acquired the pink-and-cream manor house in 1802. Already in those days, it was celebrated for its literary connections. This is where Alfred, Lord Tennyson, inspired by the lake, is said to have written Le Morte d'Arthur. Roughly around the same time, the area was the scene of some historic Lakeland skulduggery. Lanty Slee, alcohol smuggler extraordinaire, gifted with an acute business acumen, was busy in the nearby caves. High on the mountain, he was illegally distilling his much-sought-after spirits. He faced court a few times and was briefly incarcerated in Carlisle prison for his crimes.

Address Bassenthwaite Lake, CA13 9YB | Getting there From Keswick, take either
A 66 along the shoreline on the west side or A 591 along the east side, where Dodd
Wood car park is; bus 73, 554 and others from Carlisle, Calbeck and Keswick stop
at Mirehouse and in Bassenthwaite village | Access Year-round | Tip Cumbria's first
modern whisky distillery is situated near Bassenthwaite village. It produces a single malt
whisky called The Lakes Malt, along with The Lakes Vodka. Both are available for sale
(www.lakesdistillery.com).

11 St Bega's Church

It beggars belief

Bega lived in the 7th century. Or in the 9th. Or did she live at all? The story goes that she was the daughter of an Irish chieftain, and her family wanted to marry her off to a Viking prince. In order to preserve her virginity, she fled across the Irish Sea with her only possession, an arm-ring gifted to her by an angel. She landed on the English shore at St Bees, upon which the priory was founded in her honour. Whether due to Chinese whispers or miracles performed by her or her blessed bracelet, her cult endured through the millennia.

The church of St Bega, on the shore of Bassenthwaite Lake in the middle of fields, has far-reaching views of Broom Fell. Bega wanted to build a convent in a safe place, and God told her to build it on the only place that didn't have any snow. It doesn't need snow for this small, isolated church to be amazingly peaceful and tranquil. It's one of the few churches in the country that predates the first millennium and is still in use for regular services and weddings, having been restored and added to for another millennium after its construction circa 950. The large stones of its walls are a slight mystery. Are they from Roman times? If so, was the church erected on an earlier building?

Details of note are the 14th-century baptismal font, the Norman chancel arch and the prayer-story of St Bega on the north window sill. There are also simple but beautiful objects – a medieval lead crucifix and a wrought-iron hourglass used to time sermons. The main door catch is a work of art. Various local families are remembered in the stained-glass windows. Attachment and loyalty are a key concept here; the coat of arms of George II over the archway reminded people of their link to the English crown during the 1745 rebellion. There was more, but the Victorian restorations erased earlier evidence of how this little church crossed the centuries.

Address 6 The Orchard, Bassenthwaite, CA12 4QS | **Getting there** There is a pay-and-display car park at Dodd Wood on A 591. From there the church is an easy 10-minute walk by the left side of Mirehouse gardens via a public footpath and across the field. Access by car is possible, if necessary, within 50 yards of the church, down a field track with several gates to shut and open. | **Hours** Always open, services twice a month, bibles in 30 languages | **Tip** St Kentigern's at Crosthwaite is another fascinating 12th-century church, which contains a complete set of Tudor consecration crosses, nine inside and three outside. It is signposted off the B 5289 (High Hill) near Keswick (www.crosthwaitechurchkeswick.co.uk).

12 Beetham Fairy Steps
Folklore on a family walk

Cumbria heaves with myths and legends. With so many lakes, mountains and forests, there is no lack of habitat for mythical creatures. For example, the tiny, water-loving Tizzie-Whizie, a winged creature unique to Windermere, part hedgehog, part squirrel and part bee, did wonders for the Bowness tourist industry. Fairies are not shy of publicity either, they feel so much at home in the Lakes that they even 'attend' the annual fair at Fleswick Bay.

Near Beetham, you'll find Fairy Steps, a place loved by children (big and small), which can be part of a nice and easy family walk. The walk doesn't present any difficulty; it is quite short, but be aware the terrain is often muddy, so adequate footwear will be required. The fun starts as soon as you reach the woodland. Look up in trees or around bushes and you might be able to spot the first signs of fairy activity: fairy decorations in various shapes and form. It could be a fairy door or a painted stone or anything else that took the little creatures' fancy on the day.

The steps are on the Limestone Link extending from Arnside to Kirkby Lonsdale. Legend has it that the fairies use them as a means of escape when they are in danger. Being nimble, they skip all the way to the top without touching the sides. Fairies will grant you a wish if you can do the same – no need for skipping, but no touching allowed.

If your wish is not granted, you can always console yourself by admiring the spectacular panoramic views when you get to the flat grassy area at the top. Bring a picnic! It is also said that those with 'second sight' can see the fairy people. This part of the legend might be linked to the original use of these steps, which may have been a 'coffin route' similar to that near Dove Cottage (see ch. 38). Several iron rings can be seen on the rock, but there are no parish records to validate the story.

Address Hillcrest Drive, Slack Head, Milnthorpe, LA7 7BB | Getting there The best route starts from the hamlet of Hazelslack. Approaching from Silverdale, park at the lay-by near Hazelslack Farm. Cross a stile and follow the path, initially into a wood. About three-quarters of the way up are the 'pretend' fairy steps. Take them and continue following the path to your destination. | Access Year-round, slippery in rain | Tip You might want to give a magical slant to your visit to Lakeland. King Arthur is one of the most famous legends associated with Cumbria.

13_ Blea Tarn

Bucolic Blea

Blea means blue in Cumbrian dialect. This lovely little tarn from the late glacial period is remarkable in many ways. It lies high up at an altitude of 217 metres, near the meeting point of three counties – Westmorland, Cumberland and Lancashire. It's also dramatically situated in a hanging valley, which forms a pass between Little and Great Langdale valleys. The road leading to it is steep, but the reward is worth it.

On a calm day, Blea Tarn is stunning with its deep water perfectly mirroring the surroundings. This can be explained by the depth of the water. Blea is one of the deepest tarns in Lakeland; only Lake Windermere and Wastwater are deeper. It's a photographer's dream with impressive views across the water to the Langdale Pikes, and coniferous woodland to the west. Rhododendrons are also to be found in the woods. Originally from the Himalayas, the plants were introduced by the Victorians, who loved exotic flowers. All was fine until the rhododendrons escaped their manicured garden environments and headed for the hills. Soon the plants took over, and are now often treated as weeds.

In the spring and summer the shores are awash with alpine flowers. But apart from a few weekends, it can't be said that Blea Tarn is very popular with tourists. It is very much liked by ramblers, however. The circuit footpath around this very small body of water takes less than half an hour to complete. It is part of 'Miles without Stiles', a scheme suitable for pushchairs and wheelchairs. Benches are dotted along the walk and it's a good place for a picnic with the family. The night sky is among its other attractions; due to its isolated position, it is a good spot for stargazing. Blea Tarn is so special that it was chosen as the last shot in the opening montage of the BBC's 30th anniversary episode of *Countryfile*, shown at the end of July 2018.

Address LA22 9PG | Getting there The ways to Blea Tarn are steep and need careful driving. The less difficult is from Ambleside, following A 593 towards Langdale. At Skelwith Bridge, take the Chapel Stile road, pass the Old Dungeon Ghyll Hotel, where the road climbs steeply to the tarn and its car park. Bus 516 (Langdale Rambler) stops at the Old Dungeon Ghyll, 2.8 miles from the tarn. | Access Year-round, but check road conditions in winter | Tip If you walk down the path across the road from the car park there are some good vantage points almost immediately on your right. Blea Tarn is great to photograph all year round, and early mornings and later afternoons are particularly lovely.

14__Blackwell
The Arts and Crafts house

Lake shores conjure visions of aristocratic villas and beautiful gardens – very often located in sunny Italy. But Lake Windermere was once ringed with outstanding rural holiday retreats, built for wealthy Victorian businessmen and their families – a class that had no ancestral homes in which to entertain their guests. Half a dozen of these villas remain to this day. Most have been converted to luxury hotels or are now in private hands. A few have featured in films, such as Broad Leys, seen in *The French Lieutenant's Woman*. Broad Leys is now the Windermere Motor Boat Club. Blackwell, on the other hand, has been superbly restored by Lakeland Arts and is open to the public.

Blackwell was designed by Mackay Hugh Baillie Scott, an influential architect in the Arts and Crafts Movement, for Sir Edward Holt, the Mancunian brewer and Lord Mayor. Blackwell stands tall on the top of a small hill. The first thing visitors notice is the use of natural light. The house faces south, away from the views of the lake. Baillie Scott used a palette of different whites and rich hues such as bright yellow and strong green. There are stained windows in many of the rooms. Delicately carved plaster columns and carved-oak panels live in harmony, creating a joyous romantic feel.

Visitors can use an augmented reality digital application to bring to life the Holts' poignant story. Get a tablet at reception, point it at one of the family photographs and the subject will retell their story and that of Blackwell.

When Edward Holt Junior inherited Blackwell, he leased it for use as a boarding school for girls. This part of the house's story has not been omitted, and there is a dressing-up area filled with period school uniforms and broad-brimmed straw hats. It is not unusual to see little guests running around like lively visitants, equipped with the latest technology.

Address Bowness-on-Windermere, LA23 3JT, +44 (0)15394 46139, www.blackwell.org.uk, info@blackwell.org.uk | Getting there Once in Windermere, follow the signs to Bowness-on-Windermere on the B 5284. After 6 miles, turn left at a T-junction onto the A 5074 (Lyth Valley Road). Turn right where the road forks, onto the B 5360, which you can follow to Blackwell's car park. | Hours 1 Mar–31 Oct, daily 10.30am–5pm; 1 Nov–28 Feb, daily 10.30am–4pm | Tip Sizergh Castle near Kendal is another historic house worth a visit. It provides a full day out with lovely gardens.

15__ St Martin's Church

Inspiration for the American flag

On 14 June, 1777, the Second Continental Congress in Philadelphia passed a resolution establishing an official flag for the new nation of the United States: 13 stripes, alternate red and white, and 13 stars, white in a blue field. The origin of the first Stars and Stripes, which inspired songs, floated on the top of Mount Everest and was placed on the moon, wasn't recorded for posterity. But one has to admit that the legend of Betsy Ross, seamstress, manufacturing the flag to George Washington's requirements is a good story which has endured. It might be only a myth, but the tale makes sense when you visit St Martin's Church in Bowness-on-Windermere and cast your eyes on the magnificent stained-glass panel behind the altar.

George Washington, the first president of the United States, was born in 1732, in colonial Virginia, far away from the Lake District, but he is a direct descendant of John Washington, who died in Bowness in 1407. His grandmother, Mildred Warner Washington, was born in Virginia but died in Whitehaven and is buried in the grounds of St Nicholas Church cemetery there. The family coat of arms – three red stars and two red stripes on a white background – was first identified in the 12th century.

Evidence of this story can be seen in St Martin's Church if you locate the correct stained-glass window. The church, built in 1483, is located in the heart of old Bowness, surrounded by cobbled lanes. St Martin's has many glorious windows spanning the ages. One of them shows the heraldry of John Wessington (also Washington), prior of Durham Abbey, who died in 1451. The Washington coat of arms can be seen among many others in the main east stained-glass window, in the top row. There is a panel with watercolour representations of all the coats of arms by the side of the altar. Even so, spotting the correct one is tricky!

Address Lake Road, Bowness-on-Windermere, LA23 3DE, +44 (0)1539 444176, www.stmartin.org.uk, admin@stmartin.org.uk | Getting there Approaching central Bowness-on-Windermere from B 5284, the church is on your left; from A 592 / Newby Bridge it's in front of you; from A 592/Ambleside it is on the left | Hours Sun 7.30am – noon, Mon – Thu 9.30am – 1pm, Fri 9.30am – 1.30pm. Please respect worshippers. | Tip Washington is not the only president to have had a connection with the Lakes. The 28th president, Woodrow Wilson, was very fond of the area and visited five times. His ancestors were from Carlisle, where a blue plaque marking the connection can be seen at Cavendish House, Warwick Road.

16_Bowscale Tarn

The legend of the immortal talking fish

What better place than this northerly tarn hemmed by jagged crags to shut down the noise of modern life? Take a breather from the constant digital demands and travel back in time to an era when people derived pleasure from simple leisure.

Walking up to this wild and beautiful glacial mountain tarn was a popular excursion with Victorian tourists who undoubtedly were experts in exploration. Our tastes have evolved and Bowscale Tarn has fallen off the beaten track. It is now rarely visited. Victorian visitors would travel from the small village of Mungrisdale along an old peat track to reach the classic corrie tarn. The Victorian pony route can still be followed but nowadays it's more much practical to leave your car in the makeshift car park area just before the hamlet of Bowscale and start walking from there.

Much of the 5.5-mile route is a bridleway, and takes an hour and a half on average, less on the way down. If you hurry you can probably catch a cup of tea and a cake at the cottage by the road. The walk is easy, a little rough in places with a few small streams to cross. It's only when you reach the top that you can see the tarn, ringed by crags. The rolling slopes shadowing the deep water create a mysterious atmosphere. The tarn doesn't get much chance to absorb direct sunlight.

Legend has it that under the dark waters live two immortal fish, one of which has the gift of speech. You can call them or try to lure them to the surface with a song as many have tried time and time again without success. But it would appear that the best and only one way to converse with these magical creatures is to pick a very sunny day and glide in the cold waters for a spot of wild swimming. But then again, even if the immortal trout were to engage you in a conversation, the refreshing conditions and the outstanding scenery would likely leave you speechless.

Address Bowscale Tarn, Penrith, CA11 0XQ | Getting there On the A66 between Keswick and Penrith take the turn off to Mosedale, pass through Mungrisdale and the hamlet of Bowscale, look out for the car park signposted Bowscale; there is no public transport to Mosedale | Access Year-round, but check weather conditions | Tip If you love wild swimming, the Lake District offers possibilities galore for sea, tidal pools, rivers, lakes and waterfalls. Make sure to include a few sessions in your itinerary.

17 _ Caldbeck Village
The National Park's first and last village

Caldbeck is a picturesque village whose history can be traced back to before medieval times. It has the particularity to be the last (or the first) in the Lake District National Park, being very near its northern boundary. The village is also almost equidistant from Cockermouth, Keswick, Penrith and Carlisle.

Nowadays, it's often described as one of the prettiest villages in Cumbria. A shift in perspective, as in the 16th century, the focus was on the local economy. It was said that 'Caldbeck and Caldbeck Fells are worth all England else'.

The fells are rich in minerals, in total 160 different species of minerals have been identified, including copper, lead, silver and gold. Mining was a local activity as far back as the 12th century, and though the mines have now closed, a grinding stone sits in the village churchyard as a reminder. Until the turn of the 21st century, collecting was unregulated, and the fells have attracted collectors and amateur mineralogists throughout the ages. However, collecting minerals is no longer permitted without a licence.

The name Caldbeck means 'cold stream'. A path by the churchyard leads to the stream and the Howk, a limestone gorge with a waterfall. In the past, the fast-flowing water provided a power source for a large number of mills: wooden bobbins, corn, wool. Bobbin milling (see ch. 9) was a major industry in Cumbria. Priest's Mill, a former corn mill last used as a saw mill, next to the church, has been restored. The Old Brewery building was originally a corn mill, and has now been converted into private houses.

Pretty cottages are another asset to the village, take a look at the dates above their main doors. St Kentigern's (also known as St Mungo's) was heavily restored in the Victorian era but it has retained some pieces from the past such as Norman carved stones and a medieval holy water stoup.

Address Caldbeck, Wigton, CA7 8DP | Getting there Caldbeck is well signposted from the north, the road leading to the village is a turn off A 595; from the south it is a turn off A 66. | Access Year-round | Tip There are more pretty village in Lakeland than we have space to mention, Seatoller is a village of note. It was once a part of the mining industry in the 17th and 18th centuries, now the centre for climbers and walkers wishing to ascend the nearby Sky Head Pass.

18_ The Maid of Buttermere

Her beauty was her destiny

On the northern edge of the Lake District, in the village of Caldbeck, stands a 12th-century church, St Kentigern's (also known as St Mungo's). Two old headstones in its graveyard attract visitors. One reads *In Memory of Mary and Richard Harrison of Todcrofts* (see the 'Tip' for the other). Mary's story started years before she took her second husband's patronym. Baptised Mary Robinson in 1778, she was the daughter of the Fish Hotel innkeeper in Buttermere. Her fame began when she was just 15. Joseph Budworth (later Palmer), a soldier and a writer for *The Gentleman's Magazine,* remarked on her beauty in his light-hearted ramblers' guide to the lakes. Admittedly, a guidebook is a strange place in which to include a living person as a tourist attraction but that's what he did with the following words: 'Her hair was thick and long, of a dark brown, and, though unadorned with ringlets, did not seem to want them; her face was a fine oval, with full eyes, and lips as red as vermilion; her cheeks had more of the lily than the rose; … she looked an angel; and I doubt not but she is the reigning Lily of the Valley.'

As a consequence, Mary became a sensation. Five years later, she wed a gentleman claiming to be the MP for Linlithgrowshire. Her romance and her wedding to the Honorable Alexander Hope were reported in the *London Morning Post* by no less than Wordsworth's friend, Samuel Taylor Coleridge. A few people expressed doubts about such an unlikely alliance. It turned out that they were right. The man was an impersonator by the name of John Hatfield, a forger and a swindler who was already married. Convicted, he hanged a year later. Mary was heartbroken. But her popularity had grown, and she would become the subject of theatre plays, novels and poems for centuries to come. She married Richard Harrison, a local farmer, and the couple had four children. She died in 1837.

Address St Kentigern's Church, Caldbeck, Wigton, CA7 8DP | **Getting there** Follow
B 5299 into Caldbeck and the well-signposted free National Park car park, north of the
village centre, then walk back toward the village | **Access** Year-round | **Tip** John Peel, a
locally famous hunter and minor local celebrity, lies in the cemetery of St Kentigern's,
under a gravestone carved with hunting symbols. He has for company the celebrated
Maid of Buttermere.

19 Great Holker Lime

One of Britain's 50 great trees

In 2002, the Tree Council selected 50 of the great British trees in celebration of the Golden Jubilee of Her Majesty Queen Elizabeth II. The Great Holker Lime was one of them. Historically, oaks steal the thunder when it comes to legendary trees. Shakespeare immortalized one in *Macbeth*, Robin Hood and his merry band hid in another. That leaves lime trees to be talked about only for their sweet scent. In June, the lime's white flowers perfume the air in our towns. This may be why lime trees have long been a popular urban tree; Victorians were very fond of them. Note that lime trees (Tilia × europaea) have nothing to do with the citrus fruit.

According to the Holker Hall garden guide, the Great Lime Tree was 'planted in the 17th century, probably as part of a formal garden, this magnificent specimen has been carefully tended by generations of owners and gardeners. Today its huge trunk stands in a cavern formed by overhanging branches and its phenomenal girth measures an awe-inspiring 7.9 metres.' It's a little unsettling to think that a four-century-old tree springs into blossom year in, year out as if time had no impact on its living organism. A closer inspection reveals crevices where a child could hide; the branches support a mass of twigs. This protective giant imposes reverence.

A whole day can be spent visiting Holker Hall and its 25 acres of immaculately kept gardens. There are several areas, each best at different times of the year, each with its own charm. To name but a few, The Summer Garden on the site of an old tennis court was developed in the late eighties. The Neptune Cascade, completed in 1991, shows off the 17th-century Neptune statue, and lets the water flow among rhododendrons. Between the meadow and the formal gardens, there is a labyrinth inspired by a Hindu temple and Cumbrian stone circles. If this were not enough, a whole grand house awaits.

Address Cark-in-Cartmel, LA11 7PL, +44 (0)1539 558328, www.holker.co.uk, info@holker.co.uk | Getting there Approximately 5 miles south of A 590, the main road running from Kendal to Barrow-in-Furness. From M 6 (north or south), exit at J 36 and head west along A 590. From central Lake District, follow A 592 south to Newby Bridge, turn right onto A 590 and then left onto B 5278 at Haverthwaite. | Hours Mar–Oct, Wed–Sun & bank holiday Mon: hall 11am–4pm; gardens 10.30am–5pm | Tip Another quirky garden in the area is Swarthmoor Hall near Ulverston, the birthplace of Quakerism. The garden is known for its Living Quilt (www.swarthmoorhall.co.uk).

20__ Carlisle Castle

A proud gatekeeper

Back in Roman times there was a stronghold built out of earth and timber where Carlisle Castle now stands. The fortress story resonates with gory and tragic events. Through the centuries, it was fortified and re-fortified against invasions, mostly Scottish. And so, for many hundreds of years, Carlisle and its castle witnessed conflicts and sieges. Its formidable-looking portcullis symbolises its role as a gatekeeper.

The castle is probably best known as a prison, its most famous prisoner being Mary Queen of Scots, who in 1568 was imprisoned in one of the oldest parts of the castle, the Warden's Tower. This tower was later demolished. Mary and her entourage were allowed to ride and promenade outside the castle walls. This stretch is now called The Lady's Walk. Two centuries later, the Jacobites who had the misfortune to be sent to the castle didn't get the same level of comfort. They were held in the dungeons of the keep and forced to lick the walls to get a little water. The natural dips in the stone have been renamed 'licking stones'.

Guards didn't get a much better deal. The graffiti, once thought to be prisoners' carvings, may have been done by guards and soldiers, out of boredom. There is a story that describes how during some demolition work around 1830, the skeleton of a lady wearing a kilt and three rings virtually jumped out of a wall. She had been bricked in, probably still alive. Appalling enough, but 12 years later the lady reappeared in the wee hours of the morning. As the guard on duty was about to kill her, she vanished. This proved too much for the poor man who dropped dead on the spot. The castle is said to be riddled with ghosts. Two medieval soldiers live on the top floor of the keep but they don't mix with visitors. You'll be left to roam freely around the staircases, vaulted passages, chambers and ramparts.

Address Castle Way, Carlisle, CA3 8UR, +44 (0)1228 591922, www.english-heritage.org.uk/
visit/places/carlisle-castle, carlisle.castle@english-heritage.org.uk | Getting there Once in
Carlisle, follow Castle Street, at the main road (A595) there is an underpass to the castle,
and a pay-and-display car park; Carlisle is on a large railway network, the station is a
10-minute walk from the castle. | Hours Apr–Oct, daily 10am–6pm; Nov–Mar, weekends
only 10am–4pm | Tip There is a military museum attached to the castle retracing the
history of the regiments that were heavily involved in the two World Wars. It is a good place
to research ancestors who might have been part of these regiments.

21 __ Cracker Packers

'It's a Carlisle story, it's a women story'

On International Women's Day 2018, close to the McVitie's biscuit factory in Carlisle, a statue dedicated to women workers was unveiled. The workers are affectionately known locally as 'Cracker Packers'. The sculpture was commissioned by Carlisle City Council and privately funded.

Hazel Reeves is the award-winning artist responsible for the artwork. She is also known for the Emmeline Pankhurst statue in Manchester. Unlike her large bronze representation of Sir Nigel Gresley in King's Cross Station, London, the Carlisle Cracker Packers statue is small. It depicts two women standing on a Carr's Table Water cracker with the distinctive factory logo embossed onto the granite plinth below. The Cracker Packers statue is a sensitive piece, intriguing and humorous.

In 1831, Jonathan Dodgson Carr started a small bakery and biscuit factory, and within two decades it had become the largest baking business in Britain. Ever since, the Carr's biscuit factory has been an important part of Carlisle's history. It's still referred to by the name of its founder and is known as Carr's of Carlisle, in spite of a change of ownership. In 1972 the business became part of United Biscuits. Carr's biscuit factory is a remarkable phenomenon; not only was it the 'Birthplace of the Biscuit Industry', but it also was a precursor of equal opportunity. As early as the 1850s, women of Carlisle were operating on the production line. In the 1920s and 1930s, the factory was the largest local employer of women. Women were given the opportunity to work in a number of jobs, not only as packers but also as supervisors and forewomen.

The sculpture is not about Carr's but about the women who worked in the factory. It immortalises their spirit, their humour and their camaraderie. As former Cracker Packer Elsie Martley has said, 'It's a Carlisle story, it's a women story.'

Address Paddy's Market, Caldewgate, Carlisle, CA2 5TG | Getting there Large pay-and-display car park next to the castle, a 5-minute walk away along B 5307 and A 595, and the statue is in a small car park next to a bus shelter; bus 60, 60A, 61, 67, 93, 93A to the McVitie's stop; Carlisle station is served by a large number of railway lines | Access Year-round | Tip The McVitie's factory is the home of Custard Creams, of which 6.5 million are produced every day. The factory shop near the entrance is open daily 10am–4pm, where you can buy a range of biscuits and crackers.

22 First African Settlement

Rethinking Britain's immigration history

In Burgh-by-Sands, there is an uncommon memorial plaque. It reads, *The first recorded African community in Britain guarded a Roman fort on this site. 3rd century ad.* It was placed beside the gate to St Michael's church by the BBC's history unit in 2016. A complementing timeline in the churchyard, which overlies a Roman fort near the western end of Hadrian's Wall, gives visitors an insight into the important events that happened here. A replica of the plaque can be seen in the display area in the church tower.

About 500 Roman soldiers were once garrisoned at this fort, which was called Aballava ('the apple orchard'). They came from across the Roman world and included a unit that had been recruited in Morocco called the Numerus Maurorum Aurelianorum, named after emperor Aurelian. They were stationed at Burgh during the third and fourth centuries. Outside the fort was a civilian settlement where retired soldiers lived with their wives and children. So much of their blood and culture must have been African that this is considered to be the first known African community in Britain. Their presence here, in the diverse society of the Roman empire, is a reflection of our modern world.

St Michael's church was built in the 12th century, using stones from the ruins of Hadrian's Wall. Its history is unique and turbulent. In 1307, King Edward I – 'the Hammer of the Scots' – who had been on his way north to put down the rebellion led by Robert the Bruce, died in his camp north of the village. His body lay in state in the church for 10 days before being taken south.

The border warfare continued, and by 1360 the area was so dangerous that the villagers added a fortified bell tower to their church as a place of safety. The reinforced door, the spectacular heavy iron gate to the tower, and the arrow slits in its thick walls are all testimony to that time.

Address Burgh-by-Sands, CA5 6AW, www.eastsolwaychurches.org, info@eastsolwaychurches.org.uk | **Getting there** 6 miles from Carlisle, via the road towards Bowness-on-Solway. The church is in the centre of the village. Bus 93 from Carlisle runs infrequently through the day and can take almost 1.5 hours. | **Hours** Daily, including Christmas Day and New Year, summer 9am – 5pm, winter 9am – 4pm (or dusk if earlier); free guided tours Easter – 30 Sep, Fri & Sat 11am – 3pm | **Tip** Make time to walk around the village of Burgh-by-Sands and have a look at the modern statue of Edward I looking as dashing as a Hollywood actor. It was unveiled in 2007 and it is situated next to the Greyhound Inn.

23_Tullie House Museum

The old, the beautiful, the bad and the worse

Hadrian saw himself as the guardian of the Roman Empire. One of his tasks, bestowed on him by the gods, was to protect the northern boundary against the hordes of unruly local tribes. This left us a legacy of wonderful Roman artefacts which have been carefully curated by Tullie House. Visitors have been attracted to the museum's large collection for more than a century, but this doesn't imply that the display has gone stale. On the contrary, the 2015 Telegraph Family Friendly Award-winning museum has opted for an interactive approach, making for an interesting visit for a rainy day. Children can dress up as Romans before watching a video about the life of a young Roman soldier. Other galleries range from zoology to social history via a renowned collection of paintings and drawings from the seven artists who founded the Pre-Raphaelite Brotherhood, among which is a rare early watercolour by D. G. Rosetti called *Borgia*.

But maybe the most intriguing gallery is the one dedicated to the Borders and the reivers who from the late 13th century to the beginning of the 17th raided along the Anglo-Scottish border. The area was then in a constant state of guerrilla warfare. Murders, arson and pillaging ravaged the land and the economy. Reivers were irregular soldiers and reiving was a means to an end. Each side of the border was as belligerent as the other and devastating raids occurred on both sides. Some reiver words are now common in English such as 'bereave' and 'blackmail', which was then a kind of protection money. At reiver baptisms, the right hand of a male child was deliberately left un-christened so that it might deal a deadlier blow to the enemy. Reivers equipment would typically be a steel bonnet, a quilted jacket and plates of metal with an assortment of weapons, all of which can be seen in the museum, along with an audiovisual presentation.

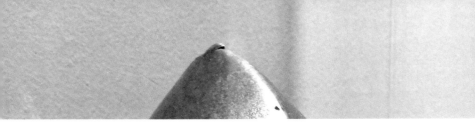

Address Castle Street, Carlisle, CA3 8TP, +44 (0)1228 618718, www.tulliehouse.co.uk, enquiries@tulliehouse.org | **Getting there** On foot from Devonshire Car Park via the road in front of Carlisle Castle, taking the underpass on the left which will bring you directly outside the main entrance; by train, Carlisle is on the London, Newcastle and Glasgow line, Tullie House is a roughly 15-minute walk from the station | **Hours** Apr–Oct, Mon–Sat 10am–5pm, Sun 11am–5pm; Nov–Mar, Mon–Sat 10am–4pm, Sun noon–4pm | **Tip** Tom Moss is a historian of the Borders. To know more about the family of reivers, head to www.reivershistory.co.uk.

24_ Turkish Baths
Moorish, and moreish Eighteenth

Eighteenth-century hammams are associated with places in the Islamic world, not exactly what you expect from a modern swimming complex in the city of Carlisle. Even more extraordinary, this beautiful Edwardian suite dedicated to health opened on 20 September, 1909, and has not changed since its construction, although the space has recently been repaired and bought up to modern standards. Carlisle Turkish Baths still have their original features and fulfil the same function today as they did in yesteryear. For a visit, a deep clean and a bit of relaxation, you'll need to leave your walking boots outside, slip into your swimming costume and head for the basement next to the swimming pool.

Designed in a flamboyant Moorish style of blue, green, cream and grey glazed brickwork, the central room is without a shadow of a doubt the masterpiece. On each of its sides are two sumptuously decorated columns. Their motifs are reproduced throughout the room. There are five changing rooms on each side and each is equipped with a lounging bed. These are separated by the original wooden screens of art nouveau panels. The centrepiece is an ice-cold plunge bath in a horseshoe shape. The bath still has its original steps and it is accessed either from the hot sauna or the even hotter steam room. It is positioned at the end of the main room, right under a beautiful arch. Natural light comes in through the windows, which are bordered by stained glass, and the speckled floor is made of terrazzo tiles.

There are only a handful of traditional Turkish baths still open in Britain, a huge contrast from the Victorian era, when every town of respectable size had to have one. London had over 100 hammams, of which only half a dozen palaces of water remain. That puts even more importance on the fact that the Carlisle Turkish Baths was recently allocated its Grade II listed status.

Address James Street, Carlisle, CA2 5AH, +44 (0)1228 810881, www.better.org.uk/leisure-centre/carlisle/the-pools | Getting there There is a car park by the leisure centre for customers using the facilities, limited to 2 hours; 10-minute walk from the train station | Hours Alternate days: gents Mon, Wed, Fri 10am–8.30pm; ladies Tue, Thu 10am–7pm; mixed Sat & Sun 9am–3pm | Tip Enough relaxing? Sports fans shouldn't leave Carlisle without attending a match or at least visiting Brunton Park, home of Carlisle United FC (www.footballgroundguide.com/leagues/england/league-two/brunton-park-carlisle-united.html).

25 Cartmel Priory

Give them bread

It is commonly said that when the monks from Bradenstoke arrived in the Cartmel area in the 12th century, they found a hill that commanded a prospect so beautiful that they decided to build their priory there. If the same monks were to time-travel to pay their home a visit in the 21st century, they would undoubtedly be wowed by the present building.

Here, there is a sense of history and harmony. The unrivalled brilliance of the medieval stained-glass windows works well with the subtle colours of the stones. The carved oak panels and the misericords from the distant past are not at odds with the contemporary sculptures by Josephina de Vasconcellos. Everything blends peacefully with everything else, in spite of the very different styles and eras. Organ music has been played in this priory since 1620, with little interruption, apart from when the first instrument was destroyed by Cromwell's army.

For all the priory's grandeur, it's the little details that are most arresting: a tiny stone guardian, half-hidden behind one of the large pillars of the Harrington Tomb as if it were playing peekaboo with the modern visitors; of course there are skulls and crossbones to depict time passing but also an hourglass to make sure we get the message and, if the St Peter's sword representation were not rare enough, what is an ear doing attached to it? So, it's almost no surprise to come across a fresh supply of bread on a shelf, on a pier near the north door. The Rowland Briggs' bread dole is an eccentric bequest dating back to 1703. Rowland Briggs, a patron of the church, left the sum of £52 to the priory in his will to pay for bread for the 'most indigent housekeepers of this parish every Sunday forever.' Quirky maybe, but it kept many parishioners from starving. The weekly loaf is still religiously placed on its shelf, but the demand is far less and the bread is seldom taken.

Address Cartmel, LA11 6QD, +44 (0)1539 536261, cartmelpriory.org.uk, info@cartmelpriory.org.uk | Getting there By car, leave M6 at junction 36, follow A591 and then A590 signposted for Barrow for about 12 miles. Shortly after passing under a footbridge, take a left turn signposted for Cartmel. The 530 Cartmel–Kendal stops at Grange-over-Sands train station, located 2.2 miles away, though it is advisable to check the timetable especially during the winter months. | Hours Mon–Sat 9am–5.30pm, Sun 9am–4.30pm; in winter, daily 9am–3.30pm | Tip Cartmel is also known for its racecourse and its two Michelin stars restaurant, L'Enclume, named the number one restaurant in the UK by *The Good Food Guide 2020*.

26 Sticky Toffee Pudding

Keeping up with the Johnses

A sticky toffee pudding is like a giant muffin made with dates then covered in rich, soft toffee sauce and served while still warm. There have been many sticky toffee puddings since its invention in the Seventies, and many chefs and cooks have tried to emulate the most renowned – Cartmel Sticky Toffee Pudding – but no one has yet succeeded to make one as deliciously moreish as that of Jean and Howard Johns.

The couple first made their version of this pudding for a restaurant they ran near Grange-over-Sands. Naturally, when they moved to Cartmel's shop-cum-post office (a beautiful example of its kind) their pudding was added to their takeaway menu. At first, they didn't make more than a few dozen for locals and tourists during high season. Though Cartmel is a lovely village, it's also very small and not really on the tourist circuit. Jean (pictured opposite) explains, 'Our pudding became very popular, very quickly and people asked where else they could get it. As a result, we packaged up some samples, this was the source of our success. We didn't invent sticky toffee pudding, we found a way to package it.' She's being modest. Everyone who has tried this delicious handmade confection will tell you that the pudding is the star, not the box it comes in.

As demand grew, the couple built a larger kitchen in their back garden, down the road from the village shop. There were regular orders from Booths, the local supermarket chain, but nothing compared to the orders following Waitrose's request to stock them. The company now employs over 30 people in order to produce over a million puddings a year, and celebrities such as Madonna have been known to order them. The little village of Cartmel ranks 44th in The *New York Times* list of the world's top travel destinations, just behind the Seychelles. Does it have sticky toffee pudding to thank? You decide.

Address Cartmel Village Shop, Parkgate House, 1 The Square, Cartmel, LA11 6QB, www.cartmelvillageshop.co.uk, nicepeople@cartmelvillageshop.co.uk | **Getting there** About a mile from A 590, there is a large pay-and-display car park on the edge of the racecourse. Getting to Cartmel by public transport is not easy but the 530 Stagecoach to Kendal stops in the village. Check the timetable, especially during the winter months. | **Hours** Mon–Sat 9am–5pm, Sun 10am–4.30pm | **Tip** The Lake District has an extensive number of local puddings. Look out for Lakeland lemon cake, Westmorland parkin, Ennerdale cake, Windermere spice biscuits and the funnily named Cumberland 'nickies' to name but a few.

27__ The History Wall

Good guys, bad guy and lots in between

There is a tradition of walls in Cumbria. Some say that it's a county of walls: Hadrian's Wall, one of the greatest walls in history, and drystone walls, which are an integral part of the scenery. The Cockermouth History Wall follows suit. The initiative originated from entrepreneur John Cusack, owner of Cockermouth Travel. The 16 panels depict stories selected from J. Bernard Bradbury's book *The History of Cockermouth*.

For a while, due to logistical problems, the project wouldn't take off. To start with, where do you build a wall without inconveniencing the existing layout of the town? Then, in 2009, came the great flood that nearly wiped out Cockermouth centre. The shopping precinct needed rebuilding. It was then or never for the History Wall. Moreover, the 70-feet-long, 8-feet-high wall is designed to act as a sturdy flood barrier, in case disaster should strike again. The History Wall was inaugurated in 2011 by Lady and Lord Bragg of Wigton, broadcaster and author.

The History Wall starts with a panel dedicated to Roman colonisation, and goes on to retell stories that have shaped the town such as the Hiring Fairs (1349–1950), Millers Footwear factory, and more. It's simultaneously a wall of fame and a wall of shame. It includes Cockermouth's famous sons; sadly it would seem that the town has so far been barren of famous daughters. Wordsworth was born in Cockermouth and his happy memories of the place greatly influenced his work; Christian Fletcher grew up on a farm nearby before taking to the seas never to return . . . after setting HMS *Bounty* on fire, off the coast of Pitcairn Island; less flamboyant but as determined was John Dalton who became a maths master at the tender age of 12 and was the first to advance a quantitative atomic theory. For a comprehensive visit and a better understanding of Cockermouth, this History Wall should be your first stop.

Address The Kings Arms Lane, Cockermouth, CA13 9LS | Getting there The wall is slightly tucked away in a lane off Main Street (B 5292), next to Boots the Chemists | Access Year-round | Tip Cockermouth's Town Trail mirrors some of the work done by local historian Bernard Bradbury. Nineteen small, numbered, cast-iron plaques were created by the children of Cockermouth School to guide visitors. An information leaflet with map is available from the Tourist Information Centre (cockermouthtouristinformationcentre@btconnect.com).

28 Squirrels Pantry

Tea? One red squirrel or two?

You would have to have a heart of stone not to smile at the sight of a red squirrel. These attractive small mammals are native to the UK. But if they have lived on these isles for 100,000 years, it has become more and more difficult to sight them, as they have become rarer. The reason for their near extinction is the arrival in 1876 of the American grey squirrels.

Grey squirrels are better competitors for food and habitat. They now occupy most of the UK territory, and only a few pockets of reds are left. Greys also carry the squirrelpox virus. A red squirrel will die within two weeks when it contracts the disease. To derail the complete demise of the native species, in 2015, a programme for their conservation was put into place. The aim is to try to maintain the population in their current stronghold areas by keeping these regions free of greys.

The North of England is such a designated area. As every little bit helps, people are put to work, asked to report sightings. To thrive, it's important that the squirrels find a constant source of food. At the Squirrels Pantry, Linda Leece and her team have been helping since the beginning of the conservation effort. The squirrels come daily for food which is put out each morning. They can appear at any time of the day, so visitors will need to be armed with patience, but as it happens Linda doesn't only feed squirrels. This gorgeous Victorian building is primarily a tea room. In the days when grey squirrels had yet to colonise the countryside, this was a potting shed and greenhouse. Now tastefully restored with parefeuille terracotta floor tiles, oak furniture and exposed red brick, the glass building is a charming tea room with a vintage feel. A hideaway where punters sample homemade cakes including Linda's Mum's sticky gingerbread and a selection of light bites such as homemade soups and fruit scones.

Address Oakhurst Garden Centre, Lamplugh Road, Cockermouth, CA13 0QN, +44 (0)1900 825873, squirrelspantry@hotmail.com | **Getting there** Situated just before the entrance to Oakhurst Garden Centre. From A66 south of Cockermouth take A5086 Lamplugh Road. Squirrels Pantry is well signposted, free car parking is available. | **Hours** Mon–Sat 9am–4pm | **Tip** Allan Bank/Grasmere, Aire Force and Ennerdale Valley are the three best places to spot red squirrels in the wild. You'll have to be patient even near feeders, as the red squirrels, unlike their arch-enemies the grey squirrels, are very shy.

29 — The Bluebird Wing
A passion for speed

The Bluebird Wing at the Ruskin Museum in Coniston is a tribute to the local hero and speed record-breaker, Donald Campbell. In the Fifties and Sixties, Campbell's eight world speed records captured the imagination of a whole generation. In 1964, he achieved a double record: 276mph on water and 403mph on land. Campbell was 45 when he died on Coniston Water, on 4 January, 1967. After a first attempt, when his famous hydroplane, Bluebird K7, almost reached the target of 300mph, Campbell tried once more. It was an attempt too far. At an estimated 320mph, Bluebird K7 went into a somersault and sank. Thirty-four years later, the hydroplane wreckage and Donald Campbell's remains were retrieved from the lake bed by diver Bill Smith and his team.

The team set out to restore the boat, and is using as much material from the original wreckage as possible. Each newly repaired part is placed on a life-size footprint of the hydroplane, in an airy room filled with natural light. One day, the completely restored hydroplane will be on display. To complete this very special tribute, there are cabinets with photographs of Campbell and mementoes such as his crash helmet.

The Ruskin Museum is owned and managed by the people of Coniston. It is built strictly on Ruskinian principles of loyalty to local materials. Slate, copper and Coniston stone were the only materials used. The buildings are low and fit in perfectly with the surroundings. In the old building, the museum celebrates John Ruskin's life. A series of rooms are crammed full of Ruskin's delicate watercolours, enchanting sketchbooks and musical instruments. Each room offers a good depiction of this leading Victorian art critic and social thinker. There is also a small room dedicated to Arthur Ransome, journalist and author, best known for his *Swallows and Amazons* series of children's adventure books.

Address Yewdale Road, Coniston, LA21 8DU, +44 (0)1539 441164, www.ruskinmuseum.com, information@ruskinmuseum.com | Getting there Coniston is a small village, with a main pay-and-display car park in the centre. There are buses to and through Coniston: Coniston Rambler 505 from Ambleside and Hawkshead, and X12 from Ulverston. The Cross Lakes Experience runs a boat/coach circuit from April to November from Windermere to Coniston. | Hours Tue–Sun 10.30am–3.30pm | Tip Ruskin's grave in the local churchyard is marked by a remarkably large, carved cross.

30__ Touchstone Fold

Art bonded to nature

Andy Goldsworthy's *Tilberthwaite Touchstone Fold* is one of a series of nearly 50 outdoor sculptures, a body of work that has been described as the biggest sculpture in the world. Cumbria County Council commissioned the ambitious series of sculptures in 1996, the Year of the Visual Arts. Goldsworthy's starting point was the changes in farming methods that led to many sheepfolds – enclosures where shepherds checked, cleaned, clipped and cared for their sheep – being left abandoned.

His proposal was to rebuild a large number of them, turning each fold into a sculpture or using it to enclose a sculpture. The sculptor worked with materials such as local slates, ancient drystone walls, trees, and old droving maps, completing the series in seven years. Each sheepfold has its own qualities, and Touchstone Fold at Tilberthwaite is mesmerising. Here, Goldsworthy used local slate and ancient drystone wall building techniques, and he incorporated his sculpture into the landscape.

The valley of Tilberthwaite, once an important centre for slate quarrying, is very picturesque with its beck and Tilberthwaite and Wetherlam fells. The first thing you see as you park are the cuts of a disused quarry in the sides of the mountains.

The large sheepfold is in the field opposite. Goldsworthy inserted a rectangle of slate into each of its four walls. In each rectangle there is a circle of slates positioned at a different angle to the wall, and reminiscent of the sun or the moon. The effect created by the sculpture is powerful. The light is collected differently by each circle so no two moments are ever the same. It doesn't matter which day of the month or which month of the year it is, the four embedded sculptures will always be illuminated differently and therefore the walls of the fold will perpetually be changing. This is a place to visit again and again.

Address Tilberthwaite, LA21 8AG, www.sheepfoldscumbria.co.uk/html/info/infox3.html or www.edenbenchmarks.org.uk/sheepfolds.htm | **Getting there** From Coniston follow A 593 toward Ambleside. The road to Tilberthwaite is on the left after about 1 mile. Follow this minor road for another mile and park in the former quarry. The fold is below the road to the right and beside the river. | **Access** Year-round | **Tip** Just to the side of the car park there are stone steps leading to Tilberthwaite Gill, an impressive rock gorge with several wonderful waterfalls, the most impressive being at the top of the gill at the start of the steep ravine.

31 Thornby Moor Dairy

A course of cheese, or a cheese-making course

Situated in Hadrian's Wall country in the Solway Plain, with the Lake District's northern fells in the background, this dairy has built a solid reputation for its production of flavoursome Cumbrian cheeses. Allerdale, Stumpies and Blue Whinnow are made at Thornby Moor using traditional skills and artisanal methods. In 1979, Carolyn Fairbairn set up a cheese dairy in the basement of the family home, using raw milk from her own herd of goats. Entirely self-taught in the craft, Allerdale was her first creation. It was produced using the time-tested trial-and-error method. Later, she experimented with cow's milk from a neighbouring farm and produced a new range. From there, the business was a step away from producing a mi-chèvre cheese – a blend of cow and goat milk. There are over 700 cheeses in the UK, but very few are produced near the Lake District.

Leonie, Carolyn's daughter, is now adding her own creativity to the family business. Her Oak Smoked Cumberland Farmhouse is a direct product of the region. The Solway Plain is good pasture land, and in the past was known for its production of butter. The inspiration behind oak-smoked cheeses is rooted in the reign of Henry VIII, when the shipbuilding industry was going strong. A large quantity of wood was required to feed the war-machine, and many oaks were planted in the north of England. Centuries later, the descendants of these trees provide the oak shavings needed to smoke the dairy's craft cheeses. The oak-smoked cheeses are easily recognisable by the burnt-orange rind.

The award-winning Thornby Moor Dairy offers the opportunity to get acquainted with the cheesemaking process. Visitors to the shop are welcome to have a look at the process during weekdays and to talk to a member of the Fairbairn family. For others who would prefer a hands-on experience, the dairy organises day courses on request.

Address Crofton Hall, Thursby, Carlisle, CA5 6QB, +44 (0)1697 345555, www.thornbymoordairy.co.uk, leonie@thornbymoordairy.co.uk | **Getting there** Take A595 from Carlisle. The dairy is the first right turn after Thursby. | **Hours** Mon–Fri 9am–5.30pm, Sat 10am–5pm | **Tip** Does your cheese need an accompaniment? The Hawkshead Relish Company is an artisan company which is known for its quality preserves, offering Lakeland relishes and chutneys using indigenous crops such as Lyth Valley damsons (www.hawksheadrelish.com).

32_ Florence Mine
A reminder of the area's mining past

As visitors turn off the A-road a mile south of the small market town of Egremont, towards Florence Mine, the earth changes colour. A deep, rusty red covers everything from flora to byroad. It gives the area a strange martian feel.

The Florence Haematite Mine is a poignant reminder of West Cumbria's industrial past. Sunk over a century ago, it provided iron ore for 50 years before being closed in 1968, following nationalisation. Soon after a nearby outfit, Beckermet Mines, took it over. The two mines worked in tandem but further rationalisation followed and in 1980, Florence Mine experienced its second closure. In a desperate attempt to save their jobs and community, the miners made a deal with British Nuclear Fuels Ltd, investing their redundancy payments in the re-opening of the pit. Egremont Mining Company was born, iron continued to provide for the mining families and BNF pumped the water out to use in their cooling systems. But, in 2007, the situation changed and Florence eventually closed. It had been active for 90 years, which made the pit the last working iron ore mine in Europe.

Today, the disused mine, with its discarded, rusting mine carts and its impressive shaft tower topped with a yellow wheel, makes the backdrop for an arts centre and a co-operative, the Florence Paintmakers. Iron has not been used on the same industrial scale for a century but surface raw iron ore is very commercial. It's a component of artists' materials from watercolours to oil paints. It's also found in cosmetics and jewellery. At the arts centre, in an adjacent studio, the Florence Paintmakers create a unique pigment called Egremont Red, available Cumbria-wide. The arts have given a new lease of life to the site, and are not restricted to visual arts. There are evenings of live music, theatre and film. Industrial art or modern art, the choice is yours.

Address Egremont, CA22 2NR, +44 (0)1946 824946, www.florenceartscentre.com, florence@glorenceartscentre.com | Getting there From M6 exit at J40, take A66 to Workington and A595 to Egremont. The mine is immediately left at the Thomas Cross roundabout, with free parking on site. Bus 30 runs from Whitehaven, Workington and Maryport. | Hours Wed–Sun 10am–4pm, from 7pm on event evenings | Tip West Cumbrian artist Colin Telfer is renowned for his sculptures covered with a mixture of resin and iron ore dust from Florence Mine. His work can be spotted all over Cumbria, with two of his sculptures commemorating iron ore mining opposite Egremont Lowes Court Gallery.

33_Monk's Bridge

Aka Matty Benn's bridge

The Lake District has a fine collection of packhorse bridges. They are easily identifiable by their narrow span, originally intended to be used by single files of horses and ponies. The low parapets allowed the panniers filled with goods to overhang. Most bridges of this kind were erected between 1650 and 1750, and understandably a lot of them have disappeared due to the harsh weather conditions, rapid rising flood waters, or simply wear and tear. But Monk's Bridge near Egremont, which was first listed only in 1967, still spans the deep rocky gorge of Friar Gill. It is said to date back to medieval times, which would make it the oldest packhorse bridge in Cumbria.

Attractive Monk's Bridge, no wider than a metre, is affectionately known locally as Matty Benn's Bridge. Nowadays it connects a remote field in Farthwaite with an open common, and is mainly used by sheep, but in the past, a crossing was of vital importance to the monks of Calder Abbey, so the church built and maintained the bridge. However, they were not the only ones to make use of the bridge; travellers and farmers did so, too.

One of them was Matty Benn, born Martha Smallwood in Egremont in 1831. Also her husband, John, and their nine children. They lived and farmed at Brackenthwaite Farm at Wilton. Some of their descendants still live locally. Matty used to bring the farm products to Boonwood's market, travelling on horseback, using pathways and bridleways. Once she had concluded her business, she would stop at the Boonwood Inn (now The Red Admiral), for a few drinks before heading back to her farm and her brood. However, it's fair to say that she might have had more than a few, as she was often spotted drunk as a lord, swaying atop her horse as it trotted over the bridge. Matty died in 1888 and is interred at Haile church cemetery.

Address South-east of Farthwaite Farmhouse, CA20 1DN | **Getting there** From A 595, between Blackbeck and Ponsonby, turn off for Calder Bridge and continue on this unnamed road for a mile to the junction of the road to Haile, Wilton and Egremont. Park by the National Trust sign for Kinniside Common. Monk's Bridge is about half a mile from here, OS grid ref. NY 06402 10261. Alternatively, use the public footpath from Calder Bridge. | **Access** Year-round; the surrounding fields can get muddy | **Tip** One of the most photogenic packhorse bridges in the Lake District is Ashness Bridge (CA12 5UN) in Borrowdale. It has Skiddaw's flanks and Bassenthwaite Lake as its backdrop.

34 Ennerdale Water
Taking the leap

Fifteen million people visit the Lake District every year, but few reach this deep glacial lake. A famous couple did – Bill Clinton and the then Hilary Rodham. In a speech, Clinton said, 'I first proposed to her on a trip to Great Britain, the first time she had been overseas. And we were on the shoreline of this wonderful little lake, Lake Ennerdale. I asked her to marry me and she said I can't do it.' Did this proposal set a trend? Perhaps, as Ennerdale Water has become a destination for leap-year proposals.

This quiet two-and-a-half-mile-long body of water with no road around it attracts another kind of starry-eyed visitor: stargazers who come to Ennerdale to stare at the Milky Way. With so few inhabitants, there is no light pollution. Fishing is another type of meditative activity that takes place on the shore of Ennerdale Water. Trout flourish in this cold environment and offer energetic anglers a good run for their money. The best fishing months are from April to June. The rare Arctic char, a relic from the Ice Age also lives in these crystal-clear deep waters. In the recent past, the species had been struggling and it had reached critical level, but it is now recovering.

Ennerdale means 'juniper valley' in ancient Norse. There is a superb gathering of fells around this body of water. The stark outlines of Pillar and Steeple, the wooded slopes of the forest of conifers, will give visitors an impression of ruggedness and a sense of wildness often associated with Scotland or Scandinavia. Wild Ennerdale Partnership has encouraged farmers to diversify; instead of the traditional sheep crowd, you might come across one of the three herds of Galloway cows, introduced recently. There are also more than 15 miles of forest roads, which are almost traffic-free and great for family cycling, though mind the potholes and practise your braking-on-gravel skills first.

Address Bowness Knott car park, CA23 3AU; Bleach Green car park, CA23 3AS | **Getting there** Approach from A 5086 Cockermouth-to-Egremont road near Cleator Moor. Follow signs to Ennerdale Bridge then choose either the north or south side of the lake. Both routes end at car parks a short distance from the shore. The nearest rail link is 7 miles away at Whitehaven; the nearest bus stops are Lamplugh and Rowrah, both about 4 miles away. | **Access** Year-round, weather permitting; for wild camping, follow the National Park Guidance (www.lakedistrict.gov.uk/visiting/wheretostay/wildcamping) | **Tip** Ennerdale woodlands is a good place to spot red squirrels. Spring and autumn are the times of the year when they are most active.

35_ Eskdale Valley

Walker's paradise

Away from the hubbub, Eskdale is a 12-mile-long valley without any lake, only a couple of tiny tarns. The population is sparse, with only three villages: Santon Bridge, Eskdale Green and Boot, home to Eskdale Mill, one of the few remaining working Lakeland corn mills. Eskdale's beauty lies in the incredible variety of its landscape. To explore the area, visitors need more than a few days; skim it and you'll be left wanting more.

Its history has been traced to the Neolithic era, 4000 years ago. Early Neolithic men built no less than five stone circles above Boot. There are remains of burial cairns, hut circles and stone-axe mining. Romans were the next people to leave traces of their passing. They built a fort on a spectacular vantage point at Hardknott. Today, vestiges of Roman edifices, built to repel bands of marauding Scots, are being dug up around Ravenglass. Next came the Vikings, followed by the Normans, then the monks of Furness Abbey who claimed most of the valley for themselves and may have opened the first iron mines. Each of these waves amended the scenery but here, nature dominates and nothing will tame the beautiful waterfall or the wooded ravines for very long.

There are several ways to explore the valley. A crowd favourite is the famous Ravenglass & Eskdale steam railway (see ch. 85), affectionately nicknamed 'La'al Ratty'. The small but perfectly formed steam engines and their carriages meander along the rivers Mite and Esk.

The Cumbrian Esk river has its head in the mountains, in the Scafells, where it takes its source. After 15 miles the river dips its feet in the sea at Ravenglass. There are many hikes suited for all levels of fitness, some ramblers making use of the steam railway to cover part of their itinerary. Even on a very busy bank holiday weekend, in Eskdale valley, it is easy to feel like a lonely explorer.

Address District postcode CA19 | **Getting there** Take M6 to J36, toward Lakes/ Windermere. Exit off A591 onto A590 for Barrow; 3 miles after Newby Bridge turn right onto A5092, then right onto A595 at Greenodd. After Broughton-in-Furness, turn right at the lights just before the River Duddon. Continue to Ulpha, cross the river, take the next left for Eskdale. Turn right at the King George IV pub and follow the lane to Boot. For a safer, longer route, stay on A595 at the traffic lights and continue to Holmbrook, then take a small lane to Irton. Turn right before Irton Hall, right at the T-junction, then left at the King George IV pub for Boot. | **Access** Year-round; not recommended for driving or walking when weather is wet/icy | **Tip** While in the area, take some time to explore Giggle Alley Japanese Garden, perfect for a family stroll (www.forestry.gov.uk/forestry/ englandcumbrianoforestgigglealley).

36__Herdwick Sheep

Ewe too

The Lake District would look very different without the iconic Herdwick sheep. These unique woolly flocks are vital to the maintenance of the landscape. Lovable 'Herdies' munch their way through virtually everything from heather to bilberry and bracken. In fact, they are often referred to as the 'gardeners of the Lake District'. This irreplaceable breed of sheep with its 'heafing' habit is perfectly suited to its environment. The lambs are taught from birth, by their mothers, which area of the mountain to stay on. There is no need for fences, they keep to their territory, also called a 'heaf'. Where any other breed would wander and probably get lost, Herdwicks will find their way back to their respective farms even in the most treacherous of weather. The Herdwicks have such a homing instinct that when a farm is sold, it is bought with the 'landlord flocks'.

If the future seems secure for the animals, it has not always been the case. This primitive breed was once threatened with extinction. Beatrix Potter, universally known for her children's books, used her position to draw attention to the problem, and her conservationist vision helped to save the breed. Beatrix Potter and her shepherd, Tom Storey, won several prizes for Herdwick breeding. When she died, she bequeathed over 4,000 acres of land and her flock to the National Trust.

Herdwicks have a distinctive look. Lambs are born black. As they mature, their fleece turns grey. The name itself derives from the Old Norse *herdvyck*. People used to speculate about their origins. Were they brought over by the rampaging Vikings or did they swim ashore from the wrecked ships of the Spanish Armada? This has been the question until recently when DNA testing was able to solve the puzzle. A primitive genome found in very few breeds suggests a common ancestral founder in the northern Orkney Islands and Scandinavia.

Address All over the Lake District fells | Tip Herdwick lamb has a unique flavour, and in 2012, Lakeland Herdwick meat was awarded Protected Designation of Origin (PDO) status. In season, it's on the local menus.

37 _ Gosforth Cross
Last Viking standing

The Gosforth Cross is a 4.5-metre-tall structure, the tallest Viking cross in England. The 10th-century red sandstone cross stands in St Mary's churchyard in the village of Gosforth. The cross is carved with scenes from Ragnarök. In Norse mythology, Ragnarök is a series of stories set in the future recounting the final struggle between the forces of evil and the Viking gods – tales of deception between good and bad deities. The saga is laced with murders such as the death of Baldr, son of Odin. Poor Baldr was an immortal and could only be killed by a mistletoe spear. At the best of times, Viking gods were a little mischievous, and they used Baldr for target practice. That gave the malicious god Loki an idea, Baldr got killed, all sorts of mayhem followed.

Besides the Viking tales, the cross also bears Christian symbols. At its top, there is a crucifix and the trinity symbol. A whole side panel is devoted to the crucifixion of Jesus. This blend of Viking saga and Christian stories reinforces the theory that Scandinavian settlers and locals once lived in enough harmony for the sort of cross-fertilization that led to the building of structures such as the Gosforth Cross.

Charles Arundel Parker, amateur antiquarian, identified the cross carvings in 1886. Once the moss and the grime were brushed away, the discovery startled many historians. But not the local minister, Reverend W. S. Calverley, who had been arguing for a long time that the structure was pagan. Parker and Calverley proceeded to continue their research together. Luckily, the area was undertaking a wave of restorations. Carved stones were being dug up in abundance, including the Fishing Stone which depicts Thor on a boat. The stone is thought to be a fragment of a second cross. Originally there would have been four tall structures of which Gosforth Cross is the last one standing.

Address St Mary's Church, Gosforth, Seascale, CA20 1AZ | Getting there St Mary's Church is on the north side of Gosforth village. From A595, take Hardingill toward Gosforth. At the first roundabout you'll see the village car park immediately on the left. Continue down Hardingill past Gosforth Bakery, and at the fork take Wasdale Road. St Mary's is on your left, 500 metres from the car park. | Access Year-round | Tip People in the know flock to Gosforth Bakery on Meadow View, CA20 1AS, to eat pies. There is a small seating area for a few people outside. The shop is very small and often has a very long queue. Their tasty lamb pie is made with Herdwick meat (Tue – Thu 6am – 3pm, Fri 6am – 2pm).

38 Dove Cottage

Daffodils are not the only flowers

Dove Cottage, outside the village of Grasmere, is probably one of the best-known places of residence in Britain. It was William Wordsworth's first family home, and is the best place in the world to see his personal belongings. William, 29, and his sister, Dorothy, 27, moved here in December 1799. After a few years, the poet married, and they were joined by his wife, Mary Hutchinson, in 1802. We know much about the Wordsworth family life thanks to Dorothy's amazing highly detailed *Grasmere Journal*.

Little has changed at Dove Cottage since Wordsworth's days, with the exception of a porch, mod cons and the sitting-room oak floorboards 'recycled' from Winchester Cathedral in 1927. It's not hard to imagine how idyllic the cottage was at first. Visitors enter through a dark vestibule, and there are four rooms of various size downstairs and four upstairs. Though no nook or cranny has been left unexplored, the house keeps some secrets such as a hole in the buttery which defies understanding.

The garden and orchard are a delight to visit, described by Wordsworth as a 'little Nook of mountain ground'. The poet wrote many of his famous poems when at Dove Cottage, including 'Daffodils', although daffodils were not Wordsworth's favourite flower; he much preferred the lesser celandine, a bright yellow star-shaped flower known as pilewort, used to treat haemorrhoids – an affliction that plagued him.

As the family grew and with a constant flow of famous literary visitors such as Coleridge, De Quincey and Walter Scott, the place became cramped. Like many dwellings back then, the home was insalubrious. Dorothy insulated the children's bedroom with sheets of newspaper, there was no running water and the toilet was outside. One of Dorothy's letters reveals, 'We are almost over-run with rats so were forced to get a cat.' In 1808, the family moved to a larger house.

...ss Wordsworth Grasmere, Town End, Grasmere, LA22 9SH | Getting there Bus 555 from and to Ambleside, Keswick or Lancaster stop opposite the cottage; pay-and-... car park nearby | Hours Daily 10am–5.30pm, last admission 5pm | Tip In 1813, the ...worths moved to Rydal Mount, above the church in Rydal, and their house is open to ...blic, with a museum and restaurant next door.

39 __ Grasmere Gingerbread Shop

The Gingerbread Woman

The Lake District has long been a foodies' paradise. Whether due to the quality of its produce or the locals' culinary ingenuity, regional products are known nationwide and appreciated abroad. Take gingerbread. Many places have a claim on spiced biscuits, but none has played such an important role for their own community as Sarah Nelson's gingerbread creation. At first glance it's a classic story of perseverance. Sarah Nelson was born Sarah Kemp in Bowness-on-Windermere, to a poor family, in 1815. Though she had little prospect of social mobility, she worked hard and soon obtained a position as a cook in a big house. She married, and the couple had three children. But, tragedy struck not once, not twice but three times. She was left childless, bereft, with a husband who was drowning his sorrows. Fortunately, by then Sarah had already created her soft, spicy and buttery gingerbread cake-cum-biscuit, which was acquiring a reputation outside the Lake District thanks to Victorian tourists.

The invention of Grasmere Gingerbread and its subsequent fame could not have been possible without the port of Whitehaven on the west coast. In the 18th and 19th centuries, Whitehaven was one of the main landing posts for sugar and spices from India and the West Indies, rivalling London and Bristol. By opening the world up to Cumbria, the goods imported gave the area its unique style of food. This in turn contributed to the development of the area's cultural identity, which led to the Lake District being awarded World Heritage status in 2017.

Sarah Nelson died at the age of 88, but her legacy lives on. Today the business is run by third-generation owners. The sweet smell wafting from the small, whitewashed, green-accented cottage attracts visitors from around the world. Be prepared to queue, but it's worth it.

Step inside the wonderful world of

The Grasmere Gingerbread®
Shop

Address Church Cottage, Grasmere, LA22 9SW, +44 (0)1539 435428,
www.grasmeregingerbread.co.uk, mailorder@grasmeregingerbread.co.uk | **Getting there**
The shop is adjacent to the medieval church of St Oswald; pay-and-display car park on
nearby Redbank Road | **Hours** Mon–Sat 9.15am–5pm, Sun 12.30–5pm | **Tip** There
are many varieties of cakes in the area. Keep an eye out for Westmorland Pepper Cake,
a fruitcake spiced with ginger, cloves and ground pepper. It fell out of favour and almost
disappeared until in 2014 the Slow Food Movement instigated its revival.

40 Loughrigg Fell Trig Point
Winning photo opportunity

Alfred Wainwright, the famous British fellwalker, described Lough-rigg Fell as a 'midget mountain'. It is a small and popular fell which peaks at 335 metres above sea level.

There are all sorts of ascents to reach the top, its triangulation pillar and superb panorama. The climb is signposted from the bottom of Rothay Park in Ambleside and is easy to follow at the beginning but, at plateau level, there is a confusion of criss-crossing paths. For this reason, if the visibility is poor or the weather about to turn, it's best to postpone the ascent. From Grasmere, the ascent requires clambering up short sections of rock, but the path is well defined. The stunning 360-degree panorama from the summit is glorious, looking down to Elterwater, Grasmere village and lake, Windermere and beyond.

Reach the Ordnance Survey triangulation pillar and you have reached the top of the fell. Loughrigg Fell triangulation pillar is one of about 6,000 'trig pillars' or 'trig points' remaining in the UK. Trig points are often concrete pillars, but Loughrigg's is a rarer stone one. They were instrumental in mapping out the shape of Great Britain, beginning in the 1930s. By positioning a theodolite, a piece of surveying equipment, on top of them, accurate angles between pairs could be measured. The 'flush bracket' found on trig points is another way to define the exact height above sea level.

That was the scientific bit. Trig points and flush brackets are quintessentially British and have found a place in the nation's psyche. While they may have fallen out of use, they are not useless. For one, they are eminently tickable and often appear on lists of best-loved objects. To reach any of them feels like an achievement. A quick look at 'trig bagging' on Instagram should be convincing evidence that these quintessentially British monuments are still the little darlings of a nation.

Address Grasmere area, Ambleside, LA22 9HQ | Getting there Park in the pay-and-display car park at Ambleside, Grasmere or White Moss Quarry. The summit can be reached from all of these places. | Access Year-round; visibility is dangerously reduced with low clouds making it easy to lose the path | Tip If you have some time, consider a detour to Rydal Cave on your way to the top of Loughrigg Fell. It is a vast, man-made quarry, which produced high-quality slate in the 19th century.

41__Money Tree

Who said money doesn't grow on trees?

Wishing wells are found across the continents. Passers-by throw a coin in a body of water in the hope that Lady Luck will grant them their wish. Money trees, into which people press coins, are rarer. Most of them are located beside popular footpaths in rural areas. Only about 200 of them have been recorded in Great Britain, one of which is on the famous Rydal-to-Grasmere 'Coffin Trail', a bridleway running through the meadows from Rydal Mount to Dove Cottage (see ch. 38). The Coffin Trail offers a variety of viewpoints and some lovely panoramas across both lakes, Grasmere and Rydal.

In the past, coffin-bearers would use flat stones for benches to rest their charge and take a breather on their way from Rydal to St Oswald in Grasmere. It's a two-hour, non-strenuous walk (as long as you're not carrying a body) with beautiful views of Rydal Water, one of the region's smallest lakes. About 30 minutes after leaving Rydal Mount, just after a little gate, you will come across the mysterious, dead, money-studded tree. It is difficult to miss – there is often a gathering around it and the studded trunk is almost on the path. Nobody knows when the bizarre custom of inserting small change in tree trunks started, only that now the Coffin Trail tree is covered with hundreds if not thousands of coins. Some are shiny; the oldest are weathered and warped.

There is a money tree in Scotland which is said to be centuries old, but this is doubtful, as these trees typically range in date from the late 18th century to the present day, and most date from the late 20th century. Moreover, if this tree had been around in Wordsworth's times, no doubt the poet or one of his fellow writers would have composed an ode to it. Since no such poem exists, nor has it been mentioned by the prolific diarist Dorothy Wordsworth, it is safe to say that the tree was alive and well in the 18th and 19th centuries.

Address Grasmere / Rydal area | Getting there Park in the pay-and-display car parks in Grasmere or near Rydal Mount. Join the bridleway starting from the back of Rydal Mount. It pops in and out of the trees. Carry on straight, ignoring all other paths, to How Top where it joins the road down to the side of Dove Cottage. From Dove Cottage the start of the path is well indicated. It's a 4-mile walk. | Access Year-round | Tip Good luck coins and magic money trees are very popular with children. If you are walking with a young family on the Coffin Trail, chances are that you'll be asked to make a wish and hammer a coin into the bark. There is another money tree on the way to Aira Force between Glenridding and Watermillock, a popular waterfall.

42 Greystoke

A king's mistress, and much more

Four miles west of Penrith, there lies the village of Greystoke, basking in a romantic glow. It offers some unusual attractions, a potter, and racing stables. To top it all off there's a pub, The Boot and Shoe, dating from 1511. A very informative board describing the history of Greystoke can be found on the way to the pub gardens. Here, you'll learn about the Black Death, the ransacking of the village church, and the various invasions of Cumbria by many armies from the Romans to the Normans, but mostly the Scottish. It makes for a fascinating read. What it doesn't tell us is how a story of love and lust gave England a family whose name was going to be known around the world: Greystoke.

King Henry I had two wives and at least ten mistresses, and fathered countless children. One of his mistresses was Edith Forn Sigulfson. When King Henry eventually tired of Edith, he married her to a noble. In view of this alliance, Edith's brother chose to join the English camp at a time when most of Cumbria was Scottish. As a result and as a recompense he retained his barony. This is how Forne of Greystoke as they were known became the Lords of Greystoke. They went on to build a castle in which 18 generations of Greystokes lived. All accounted for, none of them was ever left behind to be raised by apes in the jungles of Africa.

In 1912, Edgar Rice Burroughs, a regular visitor to Greystoke Castle, wrote *Tarzan of the Apes* using the little-known place as Tarzan's ancestral home. The charming village continued to prosper. Nicky Richards' racing stables are yet another claim to fame for the village. They bred two Grand National winners, one in 1978 and one in 1984.

The panel at the friendly Boot and Shoe concludes with the following lines: *Average life expectancy 91.3 years making Greystoke the place in England with the second longest life span.*

GREYSTOKE CAS
AND PARK
ARE NOT OPEN
THE PUBLIC

Address Greystoke, CA11 0TP, www.greystokevillage.co.uk | **Getting there** 5 miles from Penrith via B 5288. Free parking in the village. | **Access** Year-round | **Tip** Roughly 18 miles south of Greystoke is Haweswater, which appears in Sarah Hall's eponymous first novel. Sarah Hall was born and raised in Cumbria. Her fifth novel, The Wolf Border, won the 2015 Cumbria Life Culture Awards 'Writer of the Year' prize.

43_Brothers Water
A haunting name

A curious name for a lake. Brothers Water started its life as Broad Water, which is somewhat peculiar too as this body of water is not particularly large. Then, during the Victorian era, two brothers tragically drowned in an accident here, and the lake took on its current name. Situated in the north-east of the Lake District, at the northern end of the Kirkstone Pass, this is a place seldom visited. If you are after quiet parts near a picture-postcard lake, head for this little-known tarn.

Visitors start their exploring from the car park at a packhorse bridge with the unexpected name of Cow Bridge. The ancient bridge spans Goldrill Beck, and a gentle stream flows from here to the shallow lake to be met by reeds and water lilies. The surrounding fields merge with the tarn and from a little way away it looks like sheep are a fantastic amphibian breed. A small beach is situated at the south end of the lake where lily pads abound. The best time to see them in flower is July. From the car park veer left with the tarn on your left, and the walk takes you through exceptional oak woods, the likes of which there are too few left.

On the western side of the lake stands Hartsop Hall, a 16th-century Grade I listed building owned by the National Trust. The medieval building with its white walls is typical of the ancient farms in the Lake District. The farm, also owned by the National Trust, is still a working farm with a flock of sheep and a herd of Aberdeen Angus beef cattle. In an attempt to preserve the character of the lake, activities such as boating are forbidden, but it makes for a lovely picnic spot and the walking trails in the area are plentiful. Hartsop Dodd overlooks the area, resembling a cone, with an eroded top. Though steep, the path to the summit is very manageable, and as you can imagine, offers good views of the lake below.

Address Hartsop, CA11 0NZ | **Getting there** From the road leading over the Kirkstone Pass, follow A592 into Hartsop village. Cow Bridge car park is rather small; if full try along A592. | **Access** Year-round; isolated, so safest in fair weather | **Tip** Past Hartsop Hall there is an obvious track that leads to a slab bridge. From here the path starts to climb, with the Dovedale waterfalls soon visible.

44 Escape to Light

Josefina de Vasconcellos' final sculpture

In the Lake District, outdoor sculptures are common. Yet, the imposing *Escape to Light* by Josefina de Vasconcellos, located on the sand dunes between the Haverigg Inshore Rescue station and the Irish Sea, is special on several accounts. She was in her mid-90s and still active when she started to chisel it from an eight-tonne block of magnesium limestone on the grounds of Rydal Hall. *Escape to Light* is not her most emotionally charged sculpture, nor is it her most beautiful, but it is dedicated to the Independent Offshore Rescue Service. As she died before she could finish it, the work was completed by her assistants. The sculpture represents a woman with beautiful features. Her body is positioned half in, half out the jaws of a monster. Fish and seabirds populate the sides. It's weathered by the elements and it's not unusual to see children play on the massive sculpture.

Josefina Alys Hermes de Vasconcellos was a sculptor with a worldwide reputation, and a regular exhibitor at the Royal Academy. Her sculpture *Madonna and Child* is in St Paul's Cathedral in London. She was born in 1904 and died in 2005. Daughter of a Brazilian diplomat and a Quaker English mother, she married the painter and Anglican lay preacher Delmar Banner. Both loved nature and were inspired by the beauty of the Lakes. At the start of World War II, they moved to The Blied, a farmhouse in Little Langdale. The couple were close friends with Beatrix Potter. De Vasconcellos lived in Little Langdale and Ambleside until she died, aged nearly 101. Her sculptures are dotted around the Lake District, a message of faith and compassion running through them. Her internationally renowned *They Fled by Night* depicting the Holy Family can be seen in Cartmel Priory (see ch. 25) along with several more of her works. There are five moving pieces in the coastal village of St Bees.

Address Haverigg beach, LA18 4GY | Getting there The small beach of Haverigg is 2 miles from Millom. From A 595 turn onto A 5093, park in the free car park on the road which leads to the beach and walk 200 yards. By rail, from the West Coast Main Line, change at Carnforth or Preston for Millom. | Access Year-round | Tip Cumbria was and still is home to remarkable women, celebrated in various ways. To hear about the life of Harriet Martineau, the first female journalist in England (see ch. 4), go to The Armitt Museum (see ch. 3). The museum itself is named after the Armitt sisters, a talented trio across scientific and artistic fields.

45 __ Esthwaite Water

Fisher tales

This was Beatrix Potter's favourite lake and it's not difficult to see why. Esthwaite Water is one and a half miles long, and a little more than half a mile wide, and is home to the star of Potter's 1906 book, *The Tale of Jeremy Fisher*, about a frog who lives in a 'slippy-sloppy' house at the edge of the pond. Jeremy spends hours sitting on his lily-pad boat. So do Esthwaite Water fishermen, though of course their boats are not made out of lily pads.

A nature trail by the lake pays homage to Potter, who lived in the nearby 17th-century cottage called Hill Top. It's less known than its direct neighbour, Coniston, and a quieter location in which to spend time.

In 2013, the lake was listed on eBay with a price tag of £300,000 and the following description, 'A significant 280-acre lake in the heart of the Lake District with well-established leisure businesses offering a shop, a café, boating, fishing.' The Trout Fishery is the largest stocked lake in the Lake District. Fishing can take place all year round – trout throughout the season, pike in the winter, and coarse fish too; a record 46.5-pound pike was once caught here, of which pictures can be seen in the café. Self-driven boats are for rent too. The ticket office doubles as a tackle shop supplying everything required by 'the modern angler'.

Where there are fish, there are birds, and ospreys make the most of this quiet location. Electric self-driven boat safaris are organized from the boathouse. As the lake is small, it's also possible to stay on the shore and use binoculars to observe the resident ospreys fishing. Ospreys have been visiting the lake for the past decade and successfully nesting during their season from April to October; they spend the rest of the year in Africa. If you don't spot any ospreys, you'll definitely see great crested grebes, swans, ducks and oystercatchers.

Address The Boat House, Ridding Wood, Hawkshead, Ambleside, LA22 0QF, +44 (0)1539 43654, www.hawksheadtrout.com, trout@hawkshead.demon.co.uk | **Getting there** Take the car ferry from Windermere to Far Sawrey and then follow B 5285 to the lake's edge. Parking is available in the villages of Near Sawrey and Hawkshead. Pay-and-display car park on the shore of the lake at Ridding Wood. Bus 554, 555 and 556 to Hawkshead. | **Hours** The lake is accessible year-round; the boathouse is open daily 9am–6pm | **Tip** To get a bird's-eye view of Esthwaite Water, enjoy a climb to Latterbarrow, starting from Hawkshead.

46__Grizedale Forest

Giants, Ancient Foresters and Clockwork Forest

Grizedale Forest is 2,000 hectares of woodland, owned by the Forestry Commission. This is a forest for art, adventure, nature and families. There is walking, mountain biking, cycling, Segway trails, and many works of art. Visitors can fly through the trees on a zip wire, and orienteering courses of various lengths are available. The visitor centre is easy to spot with its large welcome banner, and indeed a warm welcome is given to all.

Each walking route is colour coded. Some are low-level such as the yellow low-level Millwood Trail, a short loop on a gravel-surfaced path, or the blue Ridding Wood Trail, which goes past some unusual and ornate trees. The Silurian Way is the ultimate ten-mile Grizedale walk. The trail is named after the geological time period during which the forest's characteristic grey slates were formed. The walk is categorised as 'strenuous', and it includes the Carron Crag, the highest point in the forest at 314 metres, with spectacular views. The walk passes most of the sculptures that populate the forest.

Indeed, Grizedale is famous for featuring the largest collection of site-specific artwork in the UK, the result of a collaboration between the Grizedale Society (now Grizedale Arts) and the Forestry Commission, begun in 1977. Sculptors of international renown, such as David Nash, have been included. There is no specific sculpture trail. Instead, works of art are found along the various walks. Embark on the pink Bogle Crag trail to take in Andy Goldsworthy's iconic *Taking a wall for a walk.* Each piece of art is in symbiosis with the environment and makes use of the natural surroundings. Most are carved out of wood, stone or other natural materials but not all. Some of the trail markers may be obscured by vegetation so a bit of forward planning could go a long way. Maps are available at the visitor centre, or downloadable for free.

Address Hawkshead, Ambleside, LA22 0QJ, +44 (0)300 067 4495, www.forestryengland.uk/grizedale, grizedale@forestryengland.uk | **Getting there** From the south, follow B 5286 till 2 miles after Hawkshead, then take first right and follow brown tourist signs. From the north, take A 591 to Ambleside, follow the direction to Langdale / Coniston, take B 5286 to Hawkshead then follow the signs. Parking for a fee on site. | **Hours** Visitor Centre & Forest Café, daily 10am – 4pm, summer 10am – 5pm | **Tip** If you love forest walks and mountain biking, another great destination is Whinlatter Forest (see ch. 106).

47 Honister Pass and Mine

Fasten your seat belts

The road up to the Honister Pass is a stunning scenic drive that will leave visitors panting on several counts. The road starts in Buttermere / Gatesgarth and ends in Borrowdale / Seatoller, connecting the two valleys. The mountain pass is at 356 metres above sea level, and the steep B 5289, with a gradient of 1 in 4, is a drive to remember. There are lay-bys to stop to admire the scenery or let the oncoming traffic pass.

Visitors will need to be prepared for a drastic change of weather from the valley to the top. It can be bitterly cold here and when the wind blows, it knocks people over.

The last working slate mine in England stands at the top of the pass. It's one of the very few surviving in Europe. It produces Westmorland slates, famous for covering iconic buildings such as Buckingham Palace and New Scotland Yard. The hand-polished slates come with a 300-year guarantee. The colour varies from green to turquoise, and you only need to take a look at the sculptures opposite the mine to be convinced of their beauty.

The mine was bought in 1997 by the late Mark Weir in partnership. The visionary business plan was to turn part of the quarry into an extreme tourist attraction, in order to finance the mining side of it. Visitors can watch miners in action and buy a 'Coast to Coaster' souvenir mat. If they feel adventurous on the day, they have the opportunity to walk in the footsteps of Victorian miners. To do so they'll use the via ferrata before skywalking across the Infinity Bridge more than 200 feet above the valley floor. (Via ferrata originated in the Alps, and are a system of cables, clip-on harnesses, and walkways built into the side of a mountain.) After the effort, comforting food can be bought in the five-star mine café. There is also a handy youth hostel for climbers as the pass is the starting point for the ascent of Great Gable.

Address Honister Pass, Borrowdale, Keswick, CA12 5XN, +44 (0)1768 777230, www.honister.com, info@honister.com | Getting there Follow B 5289 to the mine car park; from Easter to October bus 77/77A, also known as the Honister Rambler, makes a loop from Keswick | Hours Daily 9am–5pm; check weather and avoid windy or freezing conditions | Tip Nothing compares to the Honister experience, but some push it further by taking the Fred Whitton Challenge. The charity event consists of 112-mile cycle climbs of the Kirkstone, Honister, Newlands, Whinlatter, Hardknott and Wrynose passes. Riders complete the challenge in between 6 and 11 hours.

48__ Farrer's of Kendal

Cuppa in a TARDIS

The history of coffee is made of fabulous legends, lightly shrouded in mystery. However, we know that the first English coffee house was established in Oxford, in 1654. It is still running today; a remarkable longevity but not unique. Farrer's of Kendal, on Stricklandgate in the centre of the town, is a family business with a similar story. The company has been blending and selling teas and coffees since 1819. Coffee is no longer roasted on the premises, but with the new coffee craze engulfing England, the shop is busier than ever.

The black-and-white, double-bow-window frontage, reminiscent of another era, is very quaint. From the outside, the premises look far too small to accommodate the flow of punters going in, and one can't help wondering how they all fit.

Once inside, the layout becomes clearer. The décor is a real delight – converted gas lamps, squeaky wooden floorboards, low-beamed ceilings. The antique counter's backdrop consists of rows of large, black metal tea containers, showing only a copper-painted number. At the front, there is a display of colourful treats. A glass jar filled with small pink sugar mice from bygone times sits next to a tiny copper bell, there for attracting attention. However, it is not until a friendly member of staff takes you to a table that you realise how big this coffee house is, three storeys high with a multitude of landings.

Farrer's offers tea blends with strange and exotic names such as Formosa Oolong, Keemun, Silver Needles or Dragon Phoenix Pearl Jasmine. The company doesn't believe in 'one size fits all', which explains their long and varied coffee list. Ask for an Americano, a café au lait or a Mochaccino, and it will soon appear on your table with a complimentary biscuit. There is also a light lunch menu and a selection of cakes. This is a place without plastic trays or an internet password.

Address 13 Stricklandgate, Kendal, LA9 4LY, +44 (0)1539 731707, farrerscoffee.co.uk, sales@farrerscoffee.co.uk | Getting there Sticklandgate is in a pedestrian zone. From the north, follow A6 through to the roundabout at Kendal station, go straight ahead and follow the one-way system round the multistorey pay-on-exit car park. | Hours Mon – Sat 9am – 5.30pm | Tip Kendal Mint Cake is the original energy bar, created in 1918. It can be found in stores or direct from the Romney's factory on the Mintsfeet Industrial Estate (Kendal, LA9 6NA, www.mintcake.co.uk).

49 Kendal Climbing Wall

All-weather climbs

The word 'mountaineering' was first recorded in an 1802 letter written by the poet Samuel Taylor Coleridge to his friend William Wordsworth. In the letter Coleridge describes a tour of some of the remote parts of the Lake District along with his groundbreaking ascent of Scafell: 'I spent the greater part of the next day Mountaineering.' It took another 50 years for mountaineering to emerge as a sport. Abroad, British mountaineers were the first to reach the summit of Mount Everest. At home, with its over 200 fells, the Lake District consolidated its firm position as a favourite with climbers of all abilities.

Climbing requires skills as well as practice, so it isn't a complete surprise to find that the highest climbing wall in England is in Kendal, the town that nurtured Wainwright, the famous fell-walker. Lakeland Climbing Centre has a unique, 25-metre vertical climbing wall. The centre also offers Europe's first indoor via ferrata, and a CrazyClimb (a clip and climb activity) also known as a fun-climb. There is a whole floor that is dedicated to bouldering, where acclimatization starts. The Lakeland Climbing Centre project started in 1995 with the conversion of a disused milk drying plant on the northern edge of Kendal. A year later, Doug Scott, noted for the first ascent of the south-west face of Mount Everest, opened the centre. The centre welcomes locals and visitors, and attendance averages 200 people a day.

A few things have changed since the 19th century. Women are not considered spoilsports any more, and climbing is an inclusive sport with no divide between the sexes. The same applies to abilities. At Lakeland Climbing Centre, amateurs and famous climbers such as Leo Houlding, known for his multiple BBC shows, train together. The climbing walls also make for a visual feast, the various colours and textures resembling an abstract painting.

Address Lake District Business Park, Kendal, LA9 6NH, +44 (0)1539 721766, www.kendalwall.co.uk, info@kendalwall.co.uk | **Getting there** From the town centre, follow signs for A6 and Penrith. The centre is 1 mile or so after the train station, just before the Morrisons supermarket. | **Hours** Mon–Fri 10am–10pm, Sat & Sun 10am–6pm | **Tip** There are two other indoor climbing walls in Lakeland: Ambleside Adventure (www.amblesideadventure.co.uk) and Keswick Climbing Wall (www.keswickclimbingwall.co.uk).

50_Longsleddale

Postman Pat was born here

North of Kendal, on the eastern edge of the Lake District, lies Long-sleddale Valley, around five miles long and three miles wide. It starts at Garnett Bridge and ends with its head against the mountains at Sadgill. Framed on the west by Kentmere Pike and on the east by Sleddale Fell, with only a single road to follow, the valley is the perfect habitat for wildlife to thrive. Roe deer, red deer, badgers, rabbits, hares and red squirrels can be seen, as well as a large number of birds including lovely kingfishers by the River Sprint. The valley is sparsely populated, with the number of houses not changing since 1841. It was 30 houses then, it is 30 houses now. The area is favoured by walkers and mountain bikers, but remains a lonely spot even during peak season.

The valley, mentioned on documents dating as far back as the early 13th century, was once an important route for people and goods going to and from Scotland. The bridge at Sadgill was built in 1717 to allow travellers to cross the river. Those in need for spiritual comfort would have found a chapel near the centre of the valley. It was replaced by St Mary's Church, erected in 1863.

The valley and its inhabitants were the inspiration for John Cunliffe's story of Postman Pat. Pat first made an appearance on television in 1981, in a long-running series for pre-school children. You will not come across his red van or his black-and-white cat, but if you did, he would probably be prepared to reverse to let you pass. Pat's headquarters were based on a post office near where Cunliffe lived, and the author based his cast of distinctive inhabitants on people introduced to him by a friend.

He spent days travelling around farms to gain an insight into the life of Longsleddale dwellers. Postman Pat's Greendale is a fictitious village, but you can still hum the famous tune as you walk along the valley.

Address Longsleddale, LA8 9BB, www.longsleddale.co.uk, longsleddale@gmail.com | Getting there By car, turn north-west off A6 4 miles north of Kendal or 12 miles south of Shap. The single-lane road in the valley is not a through route. There is no mobile reception in the valley; public transport to Kentmere is sparse. | Access Year-round | Tip For visitors interested in bagging trig points, there is one on Kentmere Pike and one on Branstree. Survey pillars and benchmarks can be found too (www.longsleddale.co.uk/ pages/miscf.htm).

51 Lakeland Life & Industry

A museum in which to walk down memory fell

To understand Lakeland's present, you need to understand its past. The Museum of Lakeland Life & Industry and the Abbot Hall Art Gallery will help. Both are housed in Georgian buildings, the Abbot Hall in a grand country house and, across the courtyard, the museum in its former stables. An abstract bronze sculpture by Barbara Hepworth entitled *Oval Form (Trezion)* is the centrepiece in the courtyard. Its ovoid form with a central hole is a frequent motif of this famous northern artist.

The Museum of Lakeland Life & Industry allows visitors to walk through time exploring recreated period workshops of traditional trades such as farming, mining and tanning. Take a stroll down a Victorian high street for an immersive experience. Another gallery tells the industrial history of the Lakes and Kendal. Throughout the visit everything is in place to relive the lives of fell-dwellers and learn how this unique landscape shaped their existences. But it's not only the industrial and rural history which is retraced; creativity is not forgotten. This is the place to discover more about the life of Arthur Ransome, author of the popular children's book series, *Swallows and Amazons*, first published in 1930 but captivating children for decades though TV and cinema adaptations.

Across the yard, the Abbot Hall Art Gallery offers a permanent collection of works by Cumbrian-born artist George Romney. Romney was seen as one of the most fashionable portrait painters in the late 18th century. Emma Hamilton became his muse, and he painted over 60 portraits of her which ended up doing him no favours. He was never accepted by the art world. Besides Romney's works, the gallery boasts an impressive collection of artworks by Schwitters, Cézanne, Constable, Hockney, Moore, Picasso, Potter, Ruskin and Turner. It's one of only three places in the UK to own a Rembrandt self-portrait.

Address Kirkland, Kendal, LA9 5AL, +44 (0)1539 722464, lakelandmuseum.org.uk, info@abbothall.org.uk | Getting there Abbot Hall is beside the riverside footpath to the south of Kendal centre, with a pay-and-display car park. The nearest main-line station is Oxenholme then connect to Kendal station, a 20-minute walk from the museum. | Hours Nov–Mar, Mon–Sat 10.30am–4pm; rest of the year 10.30am–5pm | Tip You can see the sailboat Amazon, featured in Swallows and Amazons, in the Ruskin Museum in Coniston (see ch. 29).

52 Quaker Tapestry Museum
Stitched to endure

It is almost inconceivable to travel through the Lake District without coming across a reference to the Religious Society of Friends, also known as Quakers. Cumbria is the birthplace of Quakerism. George Fox's visit to Kendal in 1652 won him many followers. Quakers were influential in all areas of society: business, education, social reform and much more. Early Quaker meetings took place in private houses until 1816, when they were moved to their current location, which is also home to the Quaker Tapestry or rather, many of its panels. Some of them go on tour.

Fifteen years in the making, the tapestry panels were crafted by 4,000 men, women and children of 15 different nationalities. It is a modern creation, embroidered in the Bayeux technique between 1981 and 1989 and consisting of 77 panels chronicling 350 years of social history, Quaker ideas and experiences from the 17th century to the very recent past. Via this tapestry visitors can learn about links to companies such as Cadbury, Lloyds Bank and Clarks Shoes. It was not made to be an academic record but a celebration of Quaker ideas such as conscientious objection. The Tapestry has an artistic, historical, philosophical and local interest beside the fact that it is colourful and harmonious.

Anne Wynn-Wilson is the mastermind behind the project, and is reported to have said that the idea came to her while doing the washing-up. The panels use 120 colours and six embroidery stitches among which is 'Quaker stitch' specially designed by Anne for this project. She spent long hours analysing the look of materials and the feel of their textures. One of the panels depicts George Fox, founder of the Quaker movement. The Botanists panel is particularly delightful. It makes reference to plants and trees introduced to England by Quaker plant hunters who travelled the world to investigate them.

Address Stramongate, Kendal, LA9 4BH, +44(0)1539 722975, www.quaker-tapestry.co.uk, info@quaker-tapestry.co.uk | Getting there Friends Meeting House is very near the town centre. The nearest public car parks are a few minutes' walk away on either side of Blackhall Road. | Hours Mon–Sat 10am–5pm; closed early Dec–mid-Feb, check website for exact dates | Tip Swarthmoor Hall in Ulverston was the exact birthplace of Quakerism. It's a fully functioning Quaker centre with courses and rooms to stay (www.swarthmoorhall.co.uk).

53_ Serpentine Woods

C has a name that means one hundred feet

Serpentine Woods are a piece of local history sitting at the top of Beast Banks outside Kendal. There are three miles of footpaths, covering an Alphabet and a Nature Trail. From the start, meet *A*, a one-metre-tall, weather-beaten, carved-wood acorn. Walk a hundred metres and look up and there is *B*, a butterfly installation with beautiful wings. And so it goes.

Originally pasturage, the land was planted with trees at the end of the 18th century, and in 1824 walks were set out amongst them. The woodland became very popular very quickly and the woods suffered as a result. There is only one tree left from this period, but other Victorian features remain, including a wishing well, the Fairy Glen and a recently restored cottage. In the days when carrying a watch was the privilege of the few, Serpentine Woods were also the home of Kendal's 'time gun'. The gun was fired daily at 1.00pm, set off by electricity through the telegraph wire. The loud bang marked the workers' lunch break. The first three guns wore out, and the fourth was stolen in 1950, but its pedestal remains between the letters *R* and *Q* of the Alphabet Trail.

The Alphabet Trail was put together in 1992. A kids' quiz can be obtained from the Kendal Tourist Information Centre or the Library for a small fee. It can also be downloaded for free, and if you've left it to the last minute, there is a QR code in the woods. As the trail was never intended as a permanent exhibition, some letters have disappeared, but a new trail was developed, keeping the original letters wherever possible. Some letters are a little difficult to spot, like the *Z* for zebra which is a black-and-white picture high up in a tree. Others are interactive; you can play on *X* for xylophone. The woods are also home to a wide range of bird species, foxes and squirrels. Make sure to bring your wellies as it can get a little mucky.

Address Queen's Road, Kendal, LA9 4PD | Getting there The main entrance is halfway along Queens Road near Fellside School; free parking is available for a couple of hours on Queens Road | Access Year-round | Tip Looking for more fun foliage? Try to spot the Tebay heart-shaped wood from the M6 motorway by Tebay gorge. It was the inspiration for a song called, Heart Hill, by Kristina Olsen.

54 Bowder Stone

Did it fall or was it pushed?

Bowder Stone, which stands precariously on its edge, a 10-minute walk from the B 5289 between Grange and Rostwaite, is an estimated 2,000 tons of volcanic rock lava. It is said to be between 10 and 13 thousand years old.

Its origins are disputed. Is it a 'glacial erratic' which was carried into the area by melting glaciers or did it simply topple down from one of the sides of the valley? Nobody knows for certain, but geologists seem to favour the latter explanation since Borrowdale Valley is famous for its rocks, tumbled or not. This is probably a local stone – a very big, very impressive stone – but a peculiar one as it seems to defy gravity.

Bowder Stone has been a tourist attraction since Victorian times. Around nine metres high, it was just a matter of time before somebody with a little business sense would install a ladder to facilitate its climb. This person was Joseph Pocklington, a multimillionaire, who in 1798 purchased the land, rocks and all. He set up a crazy ladder for Victorian tourists to climb up and stand on the summit, for a penny. For another penny visitors could shake hands with the guide or a friend 'for luck' through a hole from underneath the rock – hoping that luck would hold for a little longer and the rock would not crush them. Pocklington, or 'King Pocky' as he was known by his detractors, built a small cottage next to Bowder Stone, arranged druid stones a little further on and employed old women to conjure a little bit of 'atmosphere', serve tea, sell souvenirs and postcards and act as guides.

The land on which Bowder Stone stands was the first land acquisition by the National Trust, in 1912. Nowadays, the buildings nearby are leased to the Northumbrian Mountaineering Club in order for climbers to learn their skills. The white marks visible at the bottom of the stone are left from climbing practice.

Address Grange, Keswick, CA12 5XA | Getting there There is a National Trust pay-and-display car park for the Bowder Stone, just south of Grange on B 5289; a roughly 10-minute walk on a clearly indicated walking trail leads to the stone. There are some lay-bys on the main road where you can park but they fill up early. Bus 78 from Keswick to Seatoller stops near the car park. | Access Year-round | Tip The B 5289 is a great drive from Keswick to Cockermouth, taking you over the Honister Pass (see ch. 47) past Derwent Water, through Borrowdale, past Buttermere and Crummock Water. It may be closed in the winter.

55 Catbells

Wildcat & hedgehog washerwoman

Rambling may be seen as a minority pursuit elsewhere, but not in the Lake District, and certainly not around Catbells, a lovely little mountain of 451 metres. Alfred Wainwright described it as, 'A family fell where grandmothers and infants can climb the heights together,' and people certainly do: this walk is hugely popular. The route described by Wainwright starts from the north, near Hawse End Centre for outdoor activities. During your ascent, make sure you spot the memorial plaque to Thomas Arthur Leonard, 'Father of the Open-Air Movement', who encouraged workers to go out into the countryside at a time walking and climbing was a gentleman's club. The alternative is to approach it from the south-west. It's a longer route, but your visit will take in Little Town, as well as the stunning views of Skiddaw, Derwentwater and Keswick. Little Town is indeed a tiny wee hamlet, composed of a few cottages and, a little to the south, the picturesque whitewashed Chapel of Newlands, with its beautiful stained-glass windows.

Catbells was nationally well-known prior to Wainwright's description. It was brought to fame by Beatrix Potter who made it the setting for Mrs Tiggy-Winkle's dwelling. She dedicated the story to Lucy Carr, the vicar of Newlands' daughter, with the following opening line: 'Once upon a time there was a little girl called Lucy.' Mrs Tiggy-Winkle, the hedgehog washerwoman who lived behind a little wooden door on the mountain, is not the only creature to have inhabited the area. Catbells is believed to be a distortion of 'Cat Bields'. An ancient story tells how the mountain was once home to a wild cat's den, a 'bield' in Norse.

The other way to appreciate Catbells without necessarily climbing is to admire the mountain's reflection on Derwentwater's surface. This can be done from Friar's Crag on the opposite side of the lake.

Address Keswick, CA12 5TU | **Getting there** No permanent car park at Catbells, so use the Hawse End one at Gutherscale, CA12 5UE, or park on the verge in Little Town, CA12 5TU. Visitors are advised to approach 'by bike, boots or boat'. Catch the Keswick Launch to Hawse End landing stage. Apr–Oct, bus 77A also stops at Catbells. | **Access** Year-round; avoid in bad weather | **Tip** As going to the summit is popular you might want to follow the low route along the eastern terrace towards Grange. It also commands views of Derwentwater, Keswick and the fells beyond. The walk returns along the shoreline of Derwentwater and weaves in and out of Great Bay, Abbot's Bay and Victoria Bay.

56 Centenary Stone

A stunning birthday stone

The National Trust, founded in 1895, is a charity that works to protect and preserve historic places and spaces, and plays an important part in the Lake District. Beatrix Potter was a main supporter and bequeathed her land to it. In 1995, to celebrate its centenary, the National Trust commissioned Peter Randall-Page, a British artist of international reputation, to produce an artwork for them. His creation? A birthday stone. Randall-Page took a large boulder of Borrowdale volcanic lava and sawed it in half, then placed it on the shore of Derwentwater. It has sat there ever since, sometimes in plain view, sometimes submerged. Employing his trademark organic curves, into each sheer face the artist carved a circle of 10 connected wedges – like roots, like rivers, like brains – representing a century.

To visit the stone, head towards Broomhill Point. It's a lovely flat walk of roughly 30 minutes among trees and across a field, best begun at the Lake Road car park, on the shore of Derwentwater. Take the promenade, pass the National Trust booth and the small boathouse. Just five minutes into the walk, there is a memorial to John Ruskin, who described this view from Friar's Crag as one of the three most beautiful views in Europe. The viewpoint is one of the most popular places for photographs. Continue round Standshag Bay, the first bay on the way, which makes a good spot for a picnic, and on to the second one, Calfclose Bay. The stone can't be missed but, as it is not obvious what it represents, many thousands of ramblers must have wondered about it. If only they had looked a little closer, just beside the path, they might have spotted a memorial plaque. The wood above on the left is Great Wood – another day, another walk. Red squirrels live in these parts. The animals inspired Beatrix Potter's *The Tale of Squirrel Nutkin* – another era, another work of art.

Address Calfclose Bay, Keswick, CA12 | Getting there By car from Keswick, head for the Lake Road pay-and-display car park also called Lakeside, CA12 5DJ; by launch from Keswick, go to Ashness Gate then walk south along the shore, picking up the trail here; bus 78 from Keswick to Seatoller or 77/77A, the Honister Rambler (Easter–October) | Access Year-round | Tip If the weather is poor, which let's face it, happens, why not catch a movie at The Alhambra in Keswick, a century-old cinema boasting state-of-the-art projection systems in traditional surroundings.

57_Derwent Pencil Museum
Pencil it in for a rainy day

It would be very easy to dismiss or even deride a museum dedicated to the humble pencil, coloured or not. Yet, a visit is advised before emitting an opinion on the Keswick Pencil Museum, which is not as eccentric as it sounds. Yes, it's home to the world's largest coloured (yellow) pencil, eight metres long, weighing just under half a ton. The Queen's Diamond Jubilee pencil proudly stands in a case next to miniature pencil sculptures, and the entry ticket is a wooden pencil, but most of the content is very serious. Graphite was discovered around 1500, in the nearby valley of Borrowdale, and soon became a precious commodity. A replica of the Seathwaite graphite mine, which doubles as the entrance to the museum, doesn't add much, but the next exhibition section offering videos and panels which retell the story from the start are most informative.

Take the extraordinary story of Charles Fraser-Smith, the original James Bond Q, said to have been Fleming's inspiration for the gadget-man character. The two men met at the Ministry of Supply where Fraser-Smith's job was to supply equipment and gadgets for MI6, MI9 and the Special Operations Executive (SOE). He provided anything from shaving brushes with secret compartments to edible paper. During the war, carrying a map of Germany and a compass often made the difference between life and death for RAF pilots. Fraser-Smith designed a special secret pencil kit with all the necessaries concealed in its body. Secret pencils containing escape routes and safe-house locations were also produced and sent to British prisoners of war. Nobody, especially not the enemy, found out about this ingenious secret pencil kit during the war. They were manufactured at weekends and after hours by the oldest and best-known factory, the Cumberland Pencil Company. Nowadays, they are extremely rare. The museum possesses only one example.

Address Southey Works, Keswick, CA12 5NG, +44 (0)1768 773626, www.derwentart.com/en/gb/7523/derwent-pencil-museum, derwentpencils@acco.com | **Getting there** By Greta Bridge, a short walk from the town centre and well signposted; by car from the main street, turn into Carding Mill Lane, there is a free car park in front of the museum; Keswick is a major transport hub with coaches in all directions | **Hours** Daily 9.30am–5pm | **Tip** To continue on the mine theme, visit the nearby Threlkeld Quarry and Mining Museum (www.threlkeldquarryandminingmuseum.co.uk).

58__George Fisher

If the boot fits…

In 1957, whilst a team leader with the Keswick Mountain Rescue Team, George Fisher started an outdoor equipment store in Keswick and gave it his name. George knew that in order to venture on the fells, people needed the proper equipment. Ten years later, George Fisher was becoming one of the UK's leading retailers in the field. The business won several awards, and it was around that time that it moved to its current location. In many ways, George Fisher mirrors the successes of the town it is situated in. Keswick is an attractive town that has taken advantage of its position and environment. An important wool and leather centre in the 1500s, these trades were replaced in the Victorian era by slate and graphite mines. These were in turn supplanted by tourism, but not the kind of tourism seen in the South Lakes. Walkers and climbers here are attracted by the surrounding peaks.

At George Fisher's there are still traces of the past. The famous 1880s' façade is a piece of architectural nostalgia. Don't be fooled, though; George Fisher, like Keswick, has embraced modernity. For example, behind the circular attic window is a webcam that feeds the shop website with stunning live views across Keswick to Skiddaw.

Stories of ramblers able to find perfect replacement walking boots, at short notice, are commonplace. This is in direct line with George Fisher's ethic. The now legendary personal boot-fitting service was set up for people to be safely equipped when tromping the fells. Even after Fisher retired in 1989 and the Scottish group, Tiso, took over, the Boot Room and the ethos remained the same. Feet are measured up, with and without socks. It's only after walking the test ramp, a contraption replicating the outdoors indoors, that clients are allowed to venture out on the fells or around Derwentwater, Beatrix Potter's favourite lake.

Address 2 Borrowdale Road, Keswick, CA12 5DA, +44 (0)1768 772178, www.georgefisher.co.uk, george@georgefisher.co.uk | Getting there You can park in any Keswick centre car park and walk, but the closest is off Heads Road. Walk past the Keswick Motor Company, or from the market square follow Lake Road to Borrowdale Road. | Hours Mon, Tue, Thu–Sat 9am–5.30pm, Sun 10.30am–4.30pm | Tip Keswick has a large number of good outdoor equipment shops. For a visual feast, check out @Keswickbootco on Twitter, as they publish daily photos of the area.

59__Lingholm Walled Garden

Peter Rabbit meets alpacas

Lingholm Estate may not be commonly associated with Beatrix Potter, but it was a favourite holiday destination for the Potter family, and the inspiration for some of Beatrix's best-known stories. During her youth the author spent 10 summer holidays here. All through her life, she had been reluctant to reveal the locations for her various tales, and only a year before her death did she reveal to her millions of fans that Mr McGregor's patch was in fact the 'pretty hexagonal walled garden' in Lingholm Estate. *The Tale of Peter Rabbit* was born here.

Lingholm Estate sits on the western shore of Derwentwater. Considerable groundwork took place in 2016 to clear the gardens and restore this part of the estate to an exact replica of what it looked like during the author's visits. The octagonal, walled kitchen garden was recreated on its original spot, with great success. The reference to the author's stays is far more subtle than in some of the other locations associated with her, and her work seems to blend in tastefully without taking over.

There are information panels in the garden detailing who the characters of her books were and where they came from. For example, visitors learn that cheeky Squirrel Nutkin lived around these parts in the Lingholm woodlands.

Astonishingly, a herd of alpacas has taken up residence here under the guardianship of Terry, ex-soldier, entrepreneur and aspiring pirate. Terry and Emma's herd started with a few alpacas adopted from owners who were downsizing their herd. Now, Alpacaly Ever After offers walks in the grounds, participation in feeding times and a whole range of derivative products. Sometimes life is stranger than fiction, and one can't help wondering what Beatrix Potter would have made of the real-life alpacas that can be seen going for walks in the estate or for swims in the lake.

Address Lingholm Estate, Portinscale, Keswick, CA12 5TZ, +44 (0)1768 771206, https://thelingholmkitchen.co.uk, kitchen@thelingholmestate.co.uk | **Getting there** Turn off A 66 at Portinscale, after Keswick if you come from Penrith or after the Braithwaite turning from Cockermouth. After 1.5 miles, the estate is clearly indicated, with free parking on site. Catch the Keswick Launch to Hawes End or Nichol End jetty, it's a short stroll along the footpath. On foot it's a 35-minute, flat walk from Keswick. | **Hours** Daily 9am–5pm | **Tip** There are a few alpaca farms in northern Lakeland, The Alpaca Clothing Company is one of the most original ones, with a farm, shop and café (www.thealpacaclothingco.co.uk).

60___Osprey Viewpoints
A natural reality show

Ospreys first nested beside Bassenthwaite in 2001 – the first wild ospreys to breed in the Lake District for 150 years. It had required encouragement and a lot of dedication by enthusiasts to reach this point.

The Lake District Osprey Project Partners (Forestry Commission, Lake District National Park, Royal Society for the Protection of Birds) first built a nest-platform for the fish-eating birds. It took a little time for the birds to be convinced that this was a safe environment. The team went as far as splashing the nest with a white emulsion that looks like osprey droppings. It made the platform look secure and much like an established nest. Ospreys are always curious about other osprey nests. Scottish ospreys came to visit. After all, in terms of flight, Bassenthwaite is next door.

To see the birds in action, head for Dodd Wood viewpoints reachable from the Forestry Commission car park. It's suggested to walk to the first Lower viewpoint where volunteers will give you information about the Upper viewpoint. It is a steady climb requiring a certain level of fitness. From April to August your effort will be rewarded by sightings of ospreys soaring over the woods and swooping down to the lake to fish. To get a closer look at the nest, you'll need to head for Whinlatter Visitor Centre (see ch. 106) where a webcam relays whatever is happening on the platform.

Ospreys usually mate for life and as such, there has been the same breeding pair over Bassenthwaite lake for a while now. KL, the female, has laid several clutches of eggs and the couple have raised their chicks each year. A female produces two to four eggs per season and it takes five months to raise the chicks. This is a busy time for the nest-monitoring team too, as they need to keep vigil 24/7. There are egg-collectors about. Sadly in 2018 KL didn't return. So will a new story unfold . . .?

Address Dodd Wood, Keswick, CA12 4QE, +44 (0)1768 778469, www.ospreywatch.co.uk |
Getting there 3 miles north of Keswick off the A 591, with a pay-and-display car park.
For people with reduced mobility, access to the Lower viewpoint by car can sometimes be
made by prior arrangement; call +44 (0)789 9818 421, 10am–5pm daily over the season.
By bus, take the 554 from Keswick Bus Station, alight at Mirehouse. | **Hours** Apr–Aug,
daily 10am–5pm; no staff at the viewpoint in winter | **Tip** There are over 400 birding sites
in Cumbria. There have been sightings of rare birds such as white-tailed eagles and western
cattle egrets. St Bees Head (see ch. 90) is an excellent spot to see colonies of sea birds.

61__ The Puzzling Place
See it (and have it explained) to believe it

An indoor extravaganza of puzzles and optical illusions, this attraction is similar to a giant funfair confined in a relatively small space, except that here, all the tricks are scientifically explained, and the frustration is kept to a minimum. That's once you have located the place. It's a well-hidden secret in the centre of Keswick. This is a world of illusions.

The Puzzle Area at the far end of the shop is free to enter. Here you can find unusual gadgets and give your brain a little warm-up workout before entering. The main attraction is ticketed. Be prepared for the outright spookiness of seeing static Escher woodcut snakes come to life as holograms. But by the time you reach the Hologram Gallery, you may find that nothing appears impossible. Shaking your own hand or seeing yourself as others do might not be as disorienting as you might previously have thought. Certainly not after having seen balls rolling uphill or water flowing at an unnatural angle, or having felt a little tipsy in the Anti-Gravity Room. The Ames Forced Perspective Room is the star of the show. It is the last place on the visit, the grand finale. When you look inside, from the outside, the room looks perfectly straight, but in reality, no lines are parallel. Families only have to walk across the floor for the grown-ups to shrink and the children to grow, or vice-versa. This is the only room of this kind in the country. To find another you'd have to travel to New Zealand, where the inspiration came from. Andy Willis and his brother travelled there and came back with a suitcase filled with loads of activities to trick our brains.

All of this would be a little gimmicky if there was not a perfectly logical explanation for every visual effect. The Puzzling Place makes no secret of how it all works, and the theory behind every illusion is clearly explained.

Address 9b Museum Square, Keswick, CA12 5DZ, +44 (0)1768 775102, www.puzzlingplace.co.uk, info@puzzlingplace.co.uk | Getting there Head for the pedestrianised street in the town centre and take the small street just after Blacks. The Puzzling Place is on your left mid-street above Temple Sports. There are many pay-and-display car parks in Keswick, and the town has a good network of buses but no train station. | Hours Tue–Sun, 1 Nov–20 Mar (and during school holidays) 10am–5.30pm, 21 Mar–31 Oct 11am–5.30pm | Tip Pay a visit to the Theatre by the Lake, hailed by The Independent as 'the most beautifully located and friendly theatre in England' (www.theatrebythelake.com).

62 Ruskin's View
A priceless panorama

In 2012, when Turner's watercolour known as 'Ruskin's View' was auctioned at Bonhams Auction House in London, it fetched over £215,000. The depiction of the River Lune from St Mary's Church in Kirkby Lonsdale by the famous artist had not been seen in public since 1884. In spite of its title, the painting never belonged to Ruskin, but he contributed to its fame.

John Ruskin was a 19th-century artist, an influential art critic, social theorist and husband to Effie, herself the main protagonist of one of the famous sex scandals of the time, involving Millais, a member of the Pre-Raphaelite Brotherhood. In 1875, Ruskin described the view of the Lune Valley from Kirby Longsdale's St Mary's Church, for a journal. He wrote, 'I do not know in all my own country, still less in France or Italy, a place more naturally divine, or a more priceless possession of true "Holy Land".' Soon after publication, the viewpoint became known as 'Ruskin's View'. Two centuries later, the quintessentially English panorama is still breathtaking, with the river meandering gently through meadows and woods shadowed softly by the Lake District hills. The viewpoint has a stone pulpit with a description of the sight. From the viewing platform, 86 uneven stone steps of different sizes called the Radical Steps will take you on a circular walk to the bank of the Lune, over the ancient Devil's Bridge with its three ribbed medieval arches dating back to around 1370.

One of the smallest towns in Cumbria, Kirkby Lonsdale is a pretty destination. It's a historical market town replete with references to the past, punching well above its weight. The splendid buildings dating back hundreds of years, the cobbled streets, and the Swine Market are often used as filming locations. Parts of the 'Double Sin' episode of Agatha Christie's *Poirot* and parts of Daphne du Maurier's *Jamaica Inn* were filmed here.

Address Kirkby Lonsdale, Carnforth, LA6 2BB | Getting there Enter the courtyard of St Mary the Virgin from the alleyway beside the Sun Inn, proceed to the far corner of the churchyard and follow the signs for Ruskin's View | Access Year-round | Tip The promenade and its view are part of a three-mile circle walk taking in the ancient Devil's Bridge, the Norman Church of St Mary the Virgin and the Radical Steps down to the river.

63 _ The Kirkstone Pass

Hear the boos and the wows

This is the highest road pass open to traffic in the Lake District. The four-mile ascent is gradual and on a clear day the drive has a real wow factor. In the days of coach and horses, passengers were often asked to assist the struggling animals to complete the journey by getting off and continuing on foot up to the top. It is no wonder that the road was renamed 'The Struggle'. Coachloads of tourist still flock to the top to admire the stupendous views of the surrounding lakes and valleys. At the highest point (454 metres above sea level) stands the third-highest pub in England and the highest inhabited building, The Kirkstone Pass Inn. The long, low white building has a colourful history.

The Lakes' moody weather brings many surprises, especially at this altitude. It is not difficult to believe that even ambulances on their way to assist in a heavy snowstorm get stuck. A chilling reminder is the story of poor Ruth Ray, who froze to death on her walk back from visiting her sick father in Patterdale. She joined a whole cohort of ghosts, spectres and spirits said to haunt these surroundings and spend the odd night at the inn, such as the lost hiker who plays his bag of poltergeist tricks on unsuspecting Kirkstone Inn Pass guests. Or the 17th-century coachman apparition whose photo was accidentally taken in the bar by one of his descendants. Did they take great-great-great-grandfather back home with them or did he follow them of his own accord? The story doesn't say. All we know is that he is now living with them.

For those who think that 'The Struggle' is a challenge by car or coach, spare a thought for the cyclist trying to conquer the summit. An Olympic medalist was recorded 'walking' up part of the route. A tongue-in-cheek gesture? Or maybe he was intent on admiring the commanding views of the lakes that have inspired writers and artists for centuries.

Address Windermere, LA23 1PS | Getting there On A 592 between Ullswater and Ambleside | Access Year-round; dangerous in bad weather | Tip The Kirkstone Quarry closed but if you'd like to visit a geological site and bring back a few slate-souvenirs head for the little known Threlkeld Quarry (www.threlkeldquarryandminingmuseum.co.uk).

64_ John Wilkinson Memorial

'Iron mad'

The John ('Iron-Mad') Wilkinson memorial is a huge, 12-metre-tall iron obelisk standing in a small public square by the side of the B 5277. It's a baffling monument, but so was John Wilkinson in life and even in death. Born in 1728 in Little Clifton near Workington, he was one of the great inventors of the Industrial Revolution and eventually became one of the most famous ironmasters in the world. With Abraham Darby III, he built the first iron bridge, suitably named Iron Bridge, in Broseley over the River Severn. He also invented and patented a cylinder boring machine that made cannons much more accurate and safer to fire. Probably the most outrageous of his inventions was the first iron barge, which floated successfully. At one point, his industrial empire produced a large proportion of Britain's cast iron.

By the time he died, he had two households: Castle Head in Lindale, which he shared with his wife, and another at Bradley. He shared the latter with his mistress, whom he met when he was 72. The couple had three children. In each home, there were several iron coffins. He had planned for an obelisk to stand on his grave in the grounds of Castle Head. In spite of all his preparations, everything went very wrong from the moment he died in 1808. At Bradley, the iron coffins were too small, so his body was transported to Castle Head in a wooden coffin. In the end, after many tribulations, Wilkinson was buried in one his iron coffins. However, he was interred three times, which proved to be once or twice too many, as the body was lost and has never been found. The obelisk bearing his portrait and epitaph was discarded in the undergrowth at Castle Head, later to be rescued and restored. The memorial was re-established in October 1984 where it stands now, for all to see. Next to it, there is a board telling the story of this important industrialist.

Address Lindale, Grange-over-Sands, LA11 6PA | Getting there At the village crossroads, take Lindale Hill. The monument is on the left, shortly after the roundabout, if you come from B 5277. | Access Year-round | Tip Iron Ore was mined in nearby Furness. To know more about 18th-century furnaces, visit the impressive Duddon Iron Furnace in Broughton-in-Furness.

JOHN WILKINSON,
IRON MASTER;
WHO DIED XIV JULY, MDCCCVIII;
AGED LXXX YEARS:
HIS DIFFERENT WORKS,
IN VARIOUS PARTS OF THE
KINGDOM,
ARE LASTING TESTIMONIES
OF HIS UNCEASING
LABOURS;
HIS LIFE WAS SPENT IN
ACTION
FOR THE BENEFIT
OF MAN;
AND, AS HE PRESUMED
HUMBLY TO HOPE,
TO THE
GLORY OF GOD.

65___Lacy's Caves

Wild as a hermit with fish in his hair

Near the village of Little Salkeld, directly above the Eden riverbank, five chambers are carved out of the red sandstone cliffs. Lieutenant-Colonel Samuel Lacy of Salkeld Hall commissioned the work and is said to have entertained his guests here. He even had a hermit in residence. It would be interesting to know how a Victorian gentleman formulated his party invitations for such happenings. 'See you in my pink cave where a hermit will welcome you' doesn't seem quite appropriate.

Created in an age when it was fashionable to own a romantic ruin or two, Lacy's Caves were originally surrounded by ornamental gardens. Rhododendrons and laburnums can still be seen by the forest trail that leads to the cave. The red sandstone site itself is listed as a Regionally Important Geological Site by Eden District Council. It is well maintained and there are public footpaths leading to it. In parts, the main path follows the former line connecting Long Meg Mine with the nearby Settle–Carlisle Railway. Be careful and make sure to use the old concrete path and steps, as the area is often boggy, especially if you are after that perfect picture which will require standing below the caves on the riverbank.

The walk to the caves is pleasant and relatively easy, but the area around them is narrow and can be tricky to negotiate. The woods are popular with joggers and dog-walkers so there will often be somebody to help with directions. It's a lesser known fact that Lacy's Caves is also a wild swimming spot. The River Eden is deep at that point and in the summer it's not unusual to see the local village children jump from a rock stack aptly named The Tower or use a mine shaft as a runway to leap into the river. Though if you are not an experienced wild swimmer, this is not advisable, as the river currents and the shock of the icy cold water on impact can be extremely dangerous.

Address North of Salkeld | **Getting there** Park in Little Salkeld and set off down the farm road in the direction of Lacy's Caves. Make sure to print the route from www.edenrivertrust.org.uk before setting off as the caves can be easily missed. The path is low and if it has been raining it may be cut off. | **Access** Year-round | **Tip** Cumbria is dotted with follies. Just beyond Rickerby Park on the banks of the River Eden near Carlisle, an hour's drive via the A591, there is a Victorian folly tower erected by George Head.

66 Little Salkeld Watermill
Not run-of-the-mill

'Once upon a time there was a miller who lived with his wife in great contentment…' The Grimms Brothers' words spring to mind when setting eyes on this charming watermill with its baby-pink walls and blue windows and doors, set in a peaceful atmosphere overlooking Sunnygill Beck next to the lovely village of Little Salkeld in the charming Eden Valley. Though some of the village's records go as far back as 1292, the watermill doesn't appear until the 18th century, when the Scottish army eventually left the area and the local population looked more serenely towards a peaceful future. At first, it was a small local affair. Farmers arrived with their sacks of grain to be milled. They lined up their horses and carts on the dirt road still in existence in front of the mill. Since that time, the mill has prospered only to have reversals of fortune, mirroring the ups and downs of the area. In the 1940s, when it was producing oatmeal, it ground to a halt. In 1974, the watermill was purchased and the historic wheels started grinding again.

It's one of the few mills in the UK that specialises in home-grown organic and biodynamic (BD) grains. The milling process is explained during tours where visitors can hear the miller's stories and the mill's history along with tales of the past and present village life. Bread-making courses are offered to budding and/or fully fledged bakers. There is a mill shop where visitors can buy the mill's flours, from their Harvest Flour created to be used in bread machines to a Special Blend 'invented' for vegans and vegetarians, and many more speciality flours.

Next door, there is an award-winning tearoom with two rooms serving delicious wholefood, vegetarian dishes and very nice scones. The tearoom is a welcome stop at the end of the walking circuit taking in Maughanby Circle (see ch. 67) and Lacy's Caves (see ch. 65).

Address Little Salkeld, CA10 1NN, +44 (0)1768 881523, www.organicmill.co.uk | Getting there The mill is on the C2C Cycle Route. By car or bicycle, from M6 exit at J40, follow A66 East, take A686 to Alston. After 6 miles turn left at Langwathby and follow for 1.5 miles. | Hours Mon, Tue, Thu–Sun 10.30am–4pm | Tip There are only a handful of corn mills dotted around the Lake District. Heron Mill in Beetham is an 18th-century watermill, open Wed–Sun 11am–4pm throughout the year (www.heronmill.org).

67 Maughanby Circle

A spell waiting to be broken

Stone circles have sparked the imagination of many from time immemorial. The best-known stone circle in England, Stonehenge, is turning into a commercial venue with little access for the public. Maughanby Circle, by comparison, fantastically positioned in the Cumbrian Mountains and known as 'Long Meg and Her Daughters', has been left untouched. Visitors can run around the stones feeling the grass under their feet, and there is no car park, no fences, no gift shops, as the site hardly gets visitors. Feel free to do a silly arm-flailing dance without fear of being noticed. Long Meg and Her Daughters is thought to be one of the earliest stone circles in Great Britain, dating from the early Bronze Age, and is one of the largest in Europe. It is made up of 68 or so stones, 51 of them erect, some taller than 8 feet, weighing up to 16 tonnes. Long Meg itself is a 12-foot-high block of red sandstone standing among her stone daughters. Legend has it that the stones are petrified witches, which would explain why they are not standing in a neat round circle.

It is said that on a dark night, as Long Meg, the wicked local witch, and her brood were brewing a forbidden love potion, they were spotted by Michael of Scotland, a 'good' wizard. His wrath was such that he petrified the lot on the spot. The spell can only be broken if somebody counting the number of stones on the site arrives twice at the same result. But beware of the consequences!

We will possibly never know how the stones got to where they now are or how the sites were built, nor what was their precise purpose, but Maughanby Circle has a clear astronomical alignment, especially midwinter when the sun sets over Long Meg. When gazing at the mysterious labyrinth ring symbols cut deep into Long Meg itself, visitors can't help getting a strong sense of belonging to a long line of human beings.

Address Little Salkeld, Penrith, CA10 | Getting there From Little Salkeld, head towards Glassonby. After a short distance Long Meg is signposted on the left. The stone circle is adjacent to the road where cars can be parked. | Access Year-round | Tip The stone circle of Castlerigg is situated 1.5 miles east of Keswick on the A66. The official number of stones as recorded by the National Trust is 40.

68 Wray Castle

Beatrix Potter's holiday abode

Wray Castle's brochure reads, '136 years ago a 15-year-old girl came to Wray Castle for the summer holidays with her younger brother and her parents. She recorded her adventures in a journal written in secret code so nobody else could read it. Her name was Beatrix Potter and she went on to become a famous children's author and illustrator, writing books now known worldwide like *The Tale of Peter Rabbit*.'

This Victorian Gothic Revival pile was built in the 1840s. It's cleverly designed to look like a medieval castle with arrow loops, bastions, embrasures, and the owners' coat of arms set in stone above the entrance. The more than 50 rooms positioned in the different extensions suggest additions through the centuries – a tour de force from the architect H. P. Horner to make visitors believe that the owners, James and Margaret Dawson, had a longer aristocratic lineage than was the case. The castle cost a small fortune, but Margaret was wealthy thanks to her father, a successful gin merchant. Once the castle was completed, Margaret refused point blank to live in it. For a long time, it was believed that she was plain ungrateful. In the past couple of years, the archives related to the Dawson family have been thoroughly researched and it appears that like many women throughout history, little was known about Margaret. Recently recovered documents prove that she had in fact taken great interest in the construction of her 'retirement home'.

'The ground floor of the castle is open to explore, visitors can admire Wray's church-like interiors. For safety reasons the upstairs has been temporarily shut. The views across Windermere to Ambleside with the mountains in the background are unforgettable. The walled garden and the rockery are open to the public too. People are encouraged to picnic on the lawn. Wray Castle is a good place to pretend to be kings and queens.

Address Low Wray, Ambleside, LA22 0JA, +44 (0)1539 433250, www.nationaltrust.org.uk/ wray-castle, wraycastle@nationaltrust.or.uk | Getting there By car, from the south and Bowness take the B 5285 through Hawkshead where it becomes the B 5286. Continue for 2.5 miles, then take the right turn to Wray Castle. From the north and Ambleside, take the A 593 to Clappersgate then the B 5286 toward Hawkshead. After 2.5 miles take the left turn to Wray Castle. Nearest train station is Windermere; the Green Cruise bus from Ambleside stops at Wray Castle, end Mar–end Oct only. | Hours Castle: daily 10am–4pm/5pm depending on the season; grounds: daily 8am–8pm | Tip Less well-known places associated with Beatrix Potter include: Lingholm, inspiration for Mr McGregor's garden; Newlands Valley, setting for The Tale of Mrs Tiggy-Winkle; Derwentwater, inspiration for Squirrel Nutkin and others; Moss Eccles Tarn, where Potter liked to row; The Armitt Library (see ch. 3), Hill Top, Sawrey, where she lived and worked.

69 __ Kirkstile Inn

A fine country inn, indeed

Nestled in a seldom-visited part of the Western Lakes, between Loweswater (see ch. 70) and Crummock Water, the Kirkstile Inn has been providing food and shelter to visitors for 400 years. To locate this inn, drivers will first need to spot a red telephone box, then follow a narrow country lane before casting eyes on the inn's whitewashed stone walls and black window mouldings. The building is set against the impressive volcano-shaped Melbreak Fell. The interior with its low-beamed rooms and open fires is cosy and inviting.

In spite of its secluded location, this inn is heaving with people who make the journey to this isolated spot for a pint of home-brewed Legendary Cumbrian Ale and a hearty meal; reservation is a must. The inn's brewery started in 2003 in an outbuilding with a three-barrel kit. In 2011, their Loweswater Gold was crowned Champion Golden Ale of Britain.

For the last few years, the brewery has been producing around 50 barrels of 36 gallons a week. Not all are consumed at the Kirkstile Inn. If it were the case, the owners would have to increase the number of bedrooms; as it is there are only 11. It's upstairs in the bedrooms that one can feel the wealth of history, Tudor-style, in the uneven carpeted floorboards and painted plaster walls. If only the walls could talk.

The Kirkstile Inn has a sister pub in The Dockray Hall, a historic 15th-century building in the centre of Penrith. The Hall was once home to Richard III while he was having building work done on his Penrith castle. Recently, following subsidence in the car park, some interesting mischief lying underground was uncovered. It was established that as part of the castle defences, Ralph Neville, Earl of Westmorland, had built a stone-lined tunnel to link the castle to the (now) pub. It's likely to have been used for bringing supplies or to escape if under siege.

Address Loweswater, CA13 0RU, +44 (0)1900 85219, www.kirkstile.com, info@kirkstile.com | **Getting there** From Keswick take A 66 to the Whinlatter Pass at Braithwaite. Follow B 5292 until the T-junction with B 5289. Turn left and continue for 3 miles to Loweswater. Turn left at the red telephone box and Kirkstile is 200 yards along this road. From Cockermouth take B 5289 toward Lorton. Ignore High Lorton and proceed toward Low Lorton. Continue for 3 miles following signs to Loweswater. Turn left at the same red telephone box. | **Hours** Daily, reception 8.30am – 11pm, pub 10am – 11pm, 10.30pm on Sun | **Tip** The Drunken Duck Inn is another famous country pub, in Barngates (www.drunkenduckinn.co.uk).

70__Loweswater

Untroubled waters

With the notable exception of visitors to the 400-year-old Kirkstile Inn (see ch. 69) for a chance to meet up with friends over a pint of their Cumbrian Legendary Ale, very few seem to make the trip to Loweswater. The lake, situated only seven miles from Cockermouth, is one of the least visited lakes in the region. Moreover, there is no sign of big plans looming that indicate a change.

The few who make the trip will find an unspoiled scenery of woodland, fells and grassland. The woodland of Holme Wood, which runs from the shores of the lake up the fell, is particularly impressive, boasting massive oaks, chestnuts and sycamores along with conifers. The latter has attracted a red squirrel population, which appears to have settled in. Watch for a road sign in the hamlet of Thackwaite that appears to deal with the delinquent faction of the Sciuridae family. The sign reads: *Red Squirrels Please drive slowly.*

Loweswater, 1 mile long, 800 metres wide and rather shallow, has the unique peculiarity to feed another lake. A little stream from Loweswater drains into the nearby Crummock Water, of which it was once part. Visitors can hire rowing boats from Watergate Farm, situated at the south-eastern end of the lake. Even in the midst of summer, there is no queue. The shore offers an easy, flat little circuit, a good way to breathe in the peacefulness of the surroundings. There is a good place to stop for a picnic near a small bothy on the shore.

To add a bit of excitement with a view of more turbulent waters, make a small detour to Holme Force. For hill walkers, the impressive looking Melbreak, just a mile or so away, is less of a challenge than it appears. However, we are in mountainous country here, and the high peaks always loom in the background. Red Pike, High Stile and High Crag are well known to Lake District fellwalkers.

Address Loweswater, CA13 0RU, www.visitcumbria.com/cm/loweswater-lake | Getting there From Keswick it's best to follow A 66, B 5292 and B 5289 to Lorton, then turn right into a single-track road signposted Watergate Farm, at the end of which is a car park just a few minutes' walk to the lake. From Cockermouth take B 5292 then B 5289. | Access Year-round | Tip Nearby Lorton is divided into two villages, Low and High. Mary Robinson (see ch. 18) married her imposter in St Cuthbert's, set between the two.

71_ Senhouse Roman Museum

Exquisite objects

Hadrian's Wall is the world's largest Roman artefact, stretching from Carlisle to South Shields, near Newcastle. Its 'hotspots' are interesting, but the area known as Hadrian's Wall Country that extends much further west to the coast is equally fascinating. The preservation of the Cumbrian Roman coastal heritage is in part due to the efforts of one family. As early as 1570, John Senhouse, Lord of the Manor of Ellenborough, began to collect pieces found locally. In the 18th century, Humphrey Senhouse II had a new port built, which he named Maryport, after his wife. Stones from the ruined fort of Aluna were used to erect the town, but not before having all the inscribed stones catalogued and preserved.

The collection of objects from the fort and the Roman civil settlement attached to it grew so much over the centuries that it needed its own home. The Battery, a former Royal Naval Artillery Volunteer Drill Hall built in 1885, was perfect for it. The building's location high on the cliffs provides amazing views across the Solway Firth to Scotland. Visitors can climb the platform of a reconstructed timber watchtower from where the outline of the ancient fort is visible.

The Senhouse Roman Museum collection tells many stories. Some artefacts are beautifully set into context, such as the military altars dating from 160–180 ad, which are placed against a colourful Roman street background; some have a mysterious feel to them, as is the case for the representation of a large serpent erect on a phallic stone, which could have been a grave marker. Other objects, such as jewellery and board games, help us to understand ordinary life. That's without mentioning the classic objects we all expect to see, frescoes and statues. Every single piece is highlighted and beautifully displayed. The museum won the Cumbria Tourism Visitor Attraction of the Year 2018.

Address Sea Brows, Maryport, CA15 6JD, +44 (0)1900 816168, www.senhousemuseum.co.uk, info@senhousemuseum.co.uk | Getting there The museum is on the Sea Brows at the north end of town. There is ample free parking. It's a 15-minute walk from the harbour area, following the small brown signs bearing a Roman helmet. | **Hours** Jan – Mar & Nov – Dec, Fri – Sun 10.30am – 4pm, Apr – Oct, daily 10am – 5pm; guided tours of the Roman fort Sun 2pm & 3pm | Tip Maryport is a Georgian town which has kept is character. It is worth spending time wandering around. Maybe include a visit to the Lake District Coast Aquarium (https:// coastaquarium.co.uk).

AT MARYPORT AD 160 TO A

72 __ Striding Edge

A succession of bare rocks ending in a black tower

Of the five ridges leading to the top of Helvellyn, the third-highest peak in England, the best known is Striding Edge. It's considered by many to be one of the most famous scrambles in the United Kingdom. A Grade 1 route, it's suitable for people with a good level of fitness. The breathtakingly beautiful views of Lakeland and beyond largely make up for the effort. The ridge is a narrow arête – in places it's no wider than the edge of a sharp knife. During the summer, the entire route takes 4-6 hours. During the winter's icy conditions, the ridge is dangerous, and the climb must be attempted only by experienced climbers with the correct equipment.

Artist Charles Gough should have taken this warning seriously when, in 1805, he set off to climb Striding edge with only his dog for a companion. The painter never returned. His skeleton was found three months later, with his dog still by his side and very much alive. William Wordsworth recounted these events in his poem, *Fidelity*. But it appears that the poet chose to brush quickly over the question of the dog's good health after so many days and months without sustenance, seemingly… A memorial stone to Gough that quotes part of Wordsworth's poem is to be found on Helvellyn.

Another stone tablet commemorates the attempted landing of a two-seater biplane on the steep slope leading to the escarpment as a publicity stunt. It took three tries to land finally, but the pilot barely averted disaster when taking off again. For all its terrors, Helvellyn's Striding Edge is exactly as described by Albert Wainwright, the famous fell walker, "The finest ridge there is in Lakeland." It's a very popular climb, attracting hundreds of thousands of people every year. The plateau at the summit is a favoured picnic spot, and on a clear day, you can't beat the views out to the Pennines and all the way to Scotland.

Address Walks start from Ullswater Information Centre, Beckside Car Park, CA11 0PD, +44 (0)845 901 0845, www.lakedistrict.gov.uk | **Getting there** There is a large car park at Glenridding. Begin the walk at the path by the NHS health centre, turn left and head uphill. It costs £8 to park for the full day. Bus route 508 runs from Penrith. | **Hours** Daily dawn – dusk | **Tip** For more rocky scrambling routes in the Lake District, try Blencathra via Sharp Edge, Jack's Rake up the rocky face of Pavey Ark. Both are Grade 1 scrambles.

73_ Brougham Castle & Eamont

England's birthplace

Eamont Bridge is a Late Medieval road bridge that dates back to 1425. It spans the River Eamont near the village of … you guessed it … Eamont Bridge. In spite of namesakes, it all seems rather simple, until you look at the importance of the place in England's development. The area played a pivotal role in the history of the country. In 925, several kings from all around Britain gathered near Penrith possibly in the old Roman fort to accept Athelstan as the first "King of all the English". The period is commonly regarded as the formation of England.

Multi-span bridges were common in England in medieval days but with time they were often replaced, being too narrow for modern traffic. Eamont Bridge is one of the few remaining from the 15th century. However, December 2015 saw the worst floods in living memory. The bridge was badly affected but luckily it survived, unlike the 250-year-old bridge at Pooley, which was swept away, or Brougham Old Bridge, which partly collapsed. The repairs can be seen as you look across to Brougham Castle.

The castle was built in the early 13th century by Robert de Vieuxpont, one of King John's knights. It was erected upon the foundations of Brocavum, a Roman fort, and used the fort's stones as building material. By the end of the 13th century, it had passed to the Clifford family. In the 17th century, Lady Anne Clifford, after a long battle to get her inheritance back, was instrumental in restoring the castle. Nowadays, it stands as a 'picturesque ruin'. Visitors will need all the help they can get from the Visitor Centre to make sense of its importance. The introductory exhibition includes Roman artefacts, one of which is a white sandstone altar that would clearly indicate the importance of the area for the Romans garrisoned in these parts from the year 80 until the 5th century.

Address Moor Lane, Penrith, CA10 2AA, +44 (0)1768 862488, www.english-heritage.org.uk/visit/places/brougham-castle | Getting there The very visible, well-signposted castle is situated just off the A 66 south-east of Penrith, and 1 mile from J40 on the M6, there is a lay-by opposite the castle for parking; Penrith is easily accessible by train station; bus 104 and 563 pass the castle, closest stop is Whinfell Park, be aware the A 66 is a busy road, a better option is to walk from Penrith using the path along the river. | Hours Bridge accessible all year round; castle: Apr–Sept, daily 10am–6pm; Oct, daily 10am–4pm & Nov–Mar, Sat & Sun 10am–4pm | Tip To complete the visit seek out the Countess Pillar, a brightly painted affair with four sundials erected by Lady Ann Clifford to mark the place where she said goodbye to her mother.

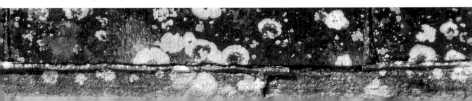

74__Brougham Hall

Home to modern arts and crafts

Brougham Hall is an early medieval building once owned by the De Burgham family, and dubbed The Windsor of the North on account of Edward VII and George V both staying here. During the 1930s, as a result of the 4th Lord Brougham losing his inheritance gambling at Monte Carlo, Brougham Hall was sold for demolition to make way for new builds. Luckily for the future of the hall, the cheque bounced. With time, the badly damaged structure eroded even more and lay in ruins until the late Christopher Terry bought it in 1985. Brougham Hall had been given a new lease of life.

On the inside line of the North Hall's walls, there is a parade of historic buildings that originally contained stables and a brewery, which are no more. Nowadays the parade is home to a dozen small businesses.

There is a wealth of talent in the arts and crafts fields in the Lake District, and Brougham Hall artisan workshops reflect just this. Home to modern creators, the place includes five potters, two painters, a jeweller, a blacksmith and a photographer, to name but a few. Brougham Hall is a good place to observe artists at work.

Pottery is an activity that has found its place in Cumbria, and Penrith is fast becoming the ceramics centre of the UK. Cumbria attracts not only local potters but international ones too. This is reflected in two annual and growing ceramics festivals: Potfest in the Park and Potfest in the Pens, which take place at Hutton-in-the-Forest and Skirsgill Auction Mart, respectively.

The Brougham Hall compound goes the extra mile too for the benefit of dogs and their owners. The complex offers families an opportunity to relax, have a bite to eat in the café, and learn a little about the history of the place. As nooks and crannies are being restored, informative boards are dotted about. On your way in or out, don't miss the famous door knocker on the courtyard gate.

Address Brougham, CA10 2DE, +44 (0)1768 868184, www.broughamhall.co.uk |
Getting there In Brougham village on B 6262 between A 6 and A 66, free parking
opposite the hall; 2 miles from Penrith station | Hours Daily, Easter – October
10am – 5pm, October – Easter 11am – 4pm | Tip 4 miles south of Penrith just off the
A 6, between Clifton and Hackthorpe villages, you'll find Abbot Lodge, a dairy farm
specialising in Jersey ice creams (www. abbottlodgejerseyicecream.co.uk).

75 __Dalemain Mansion & Gardens

Too many jars to keep under Paddington's hat

To set eyes on Dalemain Mansion and Gardens is to fall in love with the domain. Behind Dalemain's striking pink façade with its nine perfectly proportioned sash windows there is an Elizabethan manor house, a medieval hall and 'pele' tower. The initials E. H. (Edward Hasell) over the entrance are an open invitation to discover a family home like no other. The Hasell family has been living here since 1679. It is advisable to join a tour to appreciate the house and its gardens. There are so many stories to listen to – of priest holes and housekeepers, servant quarters and 18th-century hand-painted wallpaper in the Chinese Room. But explanations also help to understand the timeline. It can get a little confusing as the Edward Hasell of the front door was one of six Edward Hasells spanning the generations.

The world's original Marmalade Festival, held each March at Dalemain, was first launched in aid of local farmers during the outbreak of foot-and-mouth disease. Over a decade later, the awards have given an orange glow to hundreds of thousands of people who share a passion for marmalade. Over 2,000 competitors send their preserves to Dalemain. The success is such that the award is now also taking place in Australia and Japan.

If there ever were gardens with a soul that oozes sensibility, it is Dalemain Gardens. Visitors could spend the whole day admiring the various 'rooms' and their clever planting. Quirkiness abounds here. There is a dragon topiary, a 200-year-old tulip tree, an alphabetical herb garden for children, the largest Greek fir tree in Britain, and the blue poppies parterre for which the gardens are famous. Not only visitors fall under the spell; a few years ago, Dalemain Garden received the prestigious Garden of the Year Award from the Historic Houses Association, placing the 'manor in the valley' on par with Blenheim Palace.

Address Penrith, CA11 0HB, +44 (0)1768 486450, www.dalemain.com, marketing@dalemain.com | **Getting there** Leave M 6 at J 40, follow A 66 west to the first roundabout, then take A 592 Penrith-to-Ullswater road for 1.5 miles | **Hours** Mar–Oct, Thu–Sun, house: 10.30am–3.30pm; garden, shop, tearoom & museum: 10am– 4.30pm (garden also May–Sept, Fri 10am–4.30pm). Tours run from 10.30am. 1 Nov–14 Dec tearoom & gardens only 11am–3pm (open periods change slightly each year) | **Tip** Taste Cumbria is the county's biggest annual food and drink festival taking place in various locations throughout the year, including Kirkby Lonsdale, Ulverston, Whitehaven and Cockermouth (tastecumbria.com).

76 Giant's Grave

Viking crosses and hogback tombstones

The ancient church of St Andrew stands in the centre of Penrith. In its shadow, there are two tall, slender, carved pillars, placed five metres apart. Between the two, four low gravestones are embedded into two slabs. The low stones are known as hogbacks, a form of ancient grave monument. The ensemble is heavily worn, and it's difficult to make out what the intricate carvings looked like when the monument was erected, but there is a mysterious quality to this ancient memorial.

One would have thought that an early description of the strange edifice existed especially in view of the fact William Wordsworth and his sister, Dorothy, attended Dame Anne Birkett school, which overlooked the church. But instead, we need to turn to the author of *Robinson Crusoe*, Daniel Defoe, who in his travel diaries gives a clue of how people traditionally regarded the collection of tombstones. 'The people told us, they were the monuments of Sir Owen Caesar… but we have no inscription upon them. This Sir Owen, they tell us, was a champion of mighty strength, and of gygantick stature, and so he was, to be sure, if, as they say, he was as tall as one of the columns, and could touch both pillars with his hand at the same time.'

Indeed, nothing is really known for certain about Owain Caesarius, who was king of Cumbria from 920 to 937. There are even serious doubts about his existence, let alone his size. It is possible that this legendary king may have truly been a legend, and this makes the monument even more mysterious. The truth may lie in the words of Harriet Martineau, who in her 1855 *A Complete Guide to the English Lakes* takes a much more journalistic approach: 'In the churchyard of Penrith is the monument about which nobody really knows any thing, though it goes by the name of the Giant's Grave.' But that shouldn't stop you visiting this peaceful corner of Penrith.

Address St Andrew's Place, Penrith, CA11 7XZ, +44 (0)1768 862867 (church), www.standrewspenrith.org.uk/giantsgrave.htm, penrithparishoffice@gmail.com | Getting there Once you have parked your car in one of the town car parks, proceed towards St Andrew's either via Bishop Yards (along a row of Georgian town houses) or from Mansion House and the Rotary Garden. Penrith station is a 10-minute walk from the centre. | Access Year-round | Tip In 2004, a Viking burial ground containing 10 graves was identified by a metal detectorist near Cumwhitton, close to Carlisle, proving that Vikings had settled in the area.

77 __ Lowther Castle

Where there is a ruin, there is a way

Imagine being able to trace your ancestry to the Viking settlers who arrived in 1150. Imagine knowing you are a direct descendant of knights, earls, adventurers and business visionaries. Imagine being part of a family who have owned a large part of Cumbria since Norman times. Then imagine being offered the miserly sum of £100 for your castle and land.

This is what happened to the Honourable William James Lowther (known as Jim) after inheriting responsibility for the grand, 19th-century, Regency-Gothic, Lowther Castle. Sadly, after many tribulations, the castle was not packed with fine art, portraits and thousands-of-year-old artefacts. It was a ruin. The lawns had been covered with battery-chicken sheds and all traces of grandeur erased by the previous Lowther, the 7th Earl of Lonsdale, who at his death in 2006 left a complicated legacy stemming from four marriages. At that point, it became quite conceivable that Jim Lowther might have been tempted by the hotel conglomerate's £100 offer.

However, this was not going to be. Instead, Jim and the Lowther Estate family did something rather unusual: they decided not to restore the building but instead opted to stabilise it and concentrate the restoration efforts on the equally ruined, but historically very important, gardens. By keeping the roofless castle in its state, they have provided a magnificent ruined background to an exciting garden, lawn and land restoration. Families now come and picnic, as HRH Queen Elizabeth II and Prince Philip once did. The estate also encompasses the UK's largest wooden playground, the 'lost castle'. Opened in 2016, it is a replica of the real castle, and took some 11 miles of timber to build. The funds generated by visitors are going towards the ongoing conservation project, which includes a two-acre rose garden, proving that where there is a will, even in ruins, there is a way.

Address Lowther, Penrith, CA10 2HH, +44 (0)1931 712192, www.lowthercastle.org |
Getting there From Penrith, head for Eamont Bridge, turn right along the A 6 through
Clifton and towards Shap. At Hackthorpe turn right for Lowther village and continue
towards Askham and follow the signs for Lowther Castle. There is parking on site. | Hours
Daily, Apr–Sep 10am–5pm; Oct–Mar 10am–4pm | Tip If you haven't had enough of
castle gardens, plan a visit to Sizergh Castle near Kendal for the experience of its ancient
woodland and award-winning limestone rock garden (www.nationaltrust.org.uk/sizergh).

78__Penrith, Market Town
The 'Old Red Town' occasionally glows orange

Situated a few miles from the Lake District boundary, Penrith is a welcoming town. To pass through without exploring it would be a real shame, so slow down and stay a while. Busy and bustling, Penrith has all the charms of a historic market town, along with good rail and road links, fast internet connection and a vibrant community. Its market status dates back to 1223. For centuries, it was the place where livestock was brought for sale (see ch. 79). As such, from the Middle Ages onwards, Penrith's markets and shops have contributed to its distinct character. Today, industrial units and supermarkets support the local economy without overcrowding the town centre.

In town, tradition holds firm with drapers N. Arnison and Sons, family-run since 1742. Earlier in the 18th century this site was owned by Wordworth's grandparents. Another historic gem is J&J Graham, opened in 1793 and still going strong. True, the goods offered have changed, but it's still a deli and bakery with a range of fine food. The Toffee Shop, which has a Royal Warrant, has been making fudge and toffee since 1910. Every year, when Dalemain House holds its annual Marmalade Awards and Festival, Penrith joins in the celebrations and the town centre turns orange, including the Musgrave Monument clock tower on Market Square.

Penrith's story is depicted along the Timeline Path in the newly redesigned Coronation Garden off Portland Place. One of the four sculptures makes reference to Penrith's status as a market town. It was conceived as a deconstructed market stall and includes motifs based on the 'ten trees of Inglewood Forest', whereby newcomers to the town were allowed to fell ten oak trees to build shops and stalls. Symbols represent the seven markets mentioned on James Clarke's map of 1787: wheat, rye and potatoes, barley, oats and peas, cattle, horses, hogs.

Address Penrith, CA11 7BS | Getting there By car, exit M6 at J40, or from A1 take the A66 at Scotch Corner. By rail, Penrith rail station is a stop on several train lines with frequent service. Regular bus services depart from the station car park both to the town centre and to different parts of Cumbria including Ullswater, Windermere, Keswick and Workington. | Hours Weekly market in Cornmarket, Tue 9am–4pm; monthly farmers' market on Market Square, third Tue of each month from Mar–Dec 9.30am–2.30pm | Tip The Beacon Tower was built in 1719 to forewarn the people of Penrith of eminent danger. Its last activity dates back to the Napoleonic wars. To reach it, take a gentle climb of about a mile to get to the top of the Pike above the centre of the town.

79 _ Penrith Winter Droving

A bit of winter magic

During the winter months, it's great to put culture before nature and take refuge in one of the many towns and villages where the arrival of winter is often celebrated spectacularly. Penrith celebrates to the hilt, and their Winter Droving Festival at the end of October is a must-see. Forget Jack Frost and be prepared for an encounter with rather scary-looking Highland Cows on stilts and giant paper animals.

While the festival started in 2011 and is already a very popular date in the town's calendar, its roots are ancestral. It's a celebration of Penrith's history, when herds were led from Scotland to the south to be sold. Penrith then was at the heart of the route. Evidence of this custom can still be seen in street and pub names such as Drover's Lane or the Highland Drove.

Modern Winter Droving is a magical day of masquerade and rural celebrations ending with a spectacular torch and lantern procession. From midday, the town comes alive with street performers and music. Traditional market games take place along the streets where local food and specialities are sampled.

Competitions include a multi-skill challenge consisting of a pint-passing relay, sausage eating, hay-bale racing and egg throwing. Put together a team or join an existing one – the people of Penrith are a friendly lot – and have a go. Once it gets dark the magic continues and it's masquerade time! It looks like the entire town comes out holding torches and giant paper animal lanterns. During the procession, pride of place is given to sheep and cattle and paper fell ponies also bob about. Giant paper geese have it much easier than their real-life ancestors, which used to walk hundreds of miles to market. The journey was so arduous that their feet were coated with tar to stop them wearing out. A unicorn or two is not uncommon, though they've only ever been spotted on the doors of the Fell bar.

Address Penrith, +44 (0)1768 899444, www.winterdroving.uk, info@edenarts.co.uk | Getting there Penrith is situated just off J 40 of M 6. By train, take the West Coast Main Line. National Express operates coaches to Penrith and Stagecoach link Penrith to Carlisle and the national park. | Hours All-day festivities, torch parade early to late evening | Tip Penrith also holds a yearly farm show in July with livestock, horses, rabbits, poultry and more.

80_ Wrestling Trophies
A Cumberland and Westmorland wrestling legend

Cumberland and Westmorland wrestling is a traditional sport that has many names; Viking wrestling is one of them. Wrestling is an ancient sport dating back to early civilisation. Cave drawings in France depict wrestlers in holds that could be recognised by today's spectators. Similarly, very little has changed in the Cumberland and Westmorland wrestling world, with the notable addition of a Ladies Championship. Competitors wear traditional costumes, long johns and an embroidered vest, with a velvet centrepiece over the top. But don't be fooled by the attire, this is a noble art and novice spectators might want to get familiar with the moves and their denominations, before attending a match. The Penrith and Eden Museum is a good source of information. Here you can admire a large collection of local wrestling memorabilia; in particular, the trophies given in 1952 to the museum. The items previously belonged to the 19th-century local legend, champion wrestler of England, William Jameson. The collection is composed of nine of his belts, half a dozen silver cups and three wrestling medals, along with photographs and other visual props.

William Jameson was a Penrith native, a joiner by profession. He weighed 17 stone, and was often compared in the press to a polar bear. His gigantic stature made him a difficult man to throw, and he was also skilled and agile. His speed brought many of his opponents down. His major wins happened in 1858, and soon signalled his arrival on the big stage. However, he'd have to wait about a decade to defeat his arch-opponent Dick Wright to be crowned 'King'. In 1873, Jameson bought an inn, off Cornmarket. The acquisition was financed by his prize money and did a roaring trade with a constant stream of visiting sportsmen. The Griffin Inn is long gone, and William Jameson died in 1888. He was buried in Penrith Cemetery.

Address Middlegate, Penrith, CA11 7PT, +44 (0)1768 865105, www.eden.gov.uk/leisure-culture-and-events/penrith-and-eden-museum, museum@eden.gov.uk | **Getting there** By car, follow King Street, towards Middlegate; there is a free disc zone parking for 1 hour in front of the museum and around Penrith. The railway and coach stations in Penrith have local and national services. | **Hours** Mon–Sat 10am–5pm, Apr–Oct also Sun 11am–4pm | **Tip** Wrestling competitions take place throughout the year. To find out dates and places visit www.cumberland-westmorland-wrestling-association.com.

81 Clarkson Memorial Plaque

Viral support for Abolitionism

Thomas Clarkson, hailed as one of the heroes of the abolition of the slave trade, was born in 1760. Exhausted by his efforts in the first large-scale human rights campaign, and disappointed by its first severe defeat, he and his new wife, Catherine, 12 years his junior with political ideas of her own, withdrew to Eusemere House, a pretty cottage by a small brook, on the shore of Ullswater near Pooley Bridge. Thomas and Catherine lived in Eusemere House for 10 years. On their small estate, they grew wheat and vegetables, looked after cows and sheep, and sold their products at Penrith Market. When Catherine became ill, the couple moved back south to warmer Suffolk.

Thomas rejoined the Society for the Abolition of the Slave Trade, which he had helped establish. By then, one of the founder members, the industrialist Josiah Wedgwood, responsible for the Society's correspondence seal-design, had died. The seal showed a kneeling African in chains, lifting his hand to heaven with the words, *Am I Not a Man and a Brother?* The image went viral, reproduced on medallions, snuff boxes and coat buttons for gentlemen, bracelets and hair pins for ladies. Some were inlaid in gold. The Wedgwood Slave Emancipation design acted as an emblem for the Society.

A commissioned plaque commemorating this episode of history can be found near Eusemere House. It is based on the 18th-century Wedgwood medallion design and was created by local artist James Reynolds. Lettering is an important part of his sculptural work. The plaque is made of pigmented local black slate filled with resin giving it a smooth appearance. The lettering is different from the original, slightly recalling Roman letters, in a modernised way. The Clarkson memorial was unveiled in 2017, in the presence of Thomas and Catherine Clarkson's descendants.

Address Nearest postcode Pooley Bridge, CA10 2NR | **Getting there** Accessible only on foot or by bicycle. After the bridge in Pooley Bridge, take the path between the car park and the bridge. When you get to the lake, the memorial is on your left. Bus 508 runs from Patterdale to Penrith along the northern shore of Ullswater; Ullswater Steamer boats run from Glenridding to Pooley Bridge. There is a mainline train station in Penrith. | **Access** Year-round | **Tip** There is a new 20-mile walking route around pretty Ullswater, which helps visitors and locals to appreciate the area history via a heritage trail, highlighting farm visits, and explaining how miners, poets and political activists have shaped the area (www.ullswaterway.co.uk).

82 __ Fish Cross
Something fishy on top

Archaeological evidence shows that there have been inhabitants on the site of Pooley Bridge village since Roman times. It is even said that the area was populated before the Roman conquest. The name derives from the pool where the river meets the lake and where there was a primitive crossing.

Since the first millennium and throughout the centuries, fish has been an important part of the local industry. In the 12th century, a market charter was granted for the weekly sale of fish, in the market square. The latter was marked by a cross monument with a fish and a weather vane similar to the one you see today. Fish traps were in place between the river and the lake by the 18th-century bridge. Sadly, the bridge is no more; it was swept away by the 2015 floods. At the end of the 18th century the census records 237 inhabitants in Pooley. With the growth of tourism, however, the cross was seen as a traffic impediment, so it was removed in 1859 to make way for turning stagecoaches.

Wanting to mark the arrival of the 21st century, the Barton Parish Council, after a fair bit of controversy, settled on a monument that would commemorate the granting of the charter and highlight the village's fishing connections. The Millennium monument designed by James Banks stands in Crown Square. It is a four-metre-high, pink sandstone column and incorporates Pooley Bridge history. It's also a reminder that in the past there was a cross here in Pooley. The tall pedestal is situated on Crown Square, topped with a two-metre obelisk on which a silver metal weathervane sits. There is a silver fish on top. The Coats of Arms of the Dacres and Hasells of Dalemain families are etched on two of the monument faces. This is in recognition of the historical role both families played in the area. Bizarrely, because of its height, the silver fish at the top can often go unnoticed.

Address Crown Square, Pooley Bridge, CA10 2NW | Getting there By car, from A 66 take A 592 and B 5320. There is a car park in the village, on the right just after the bridge, and a row of parking spaces on the left by the Fish Cross; bus 508 from Windermere to Penrith stops at the Crown Hotel. | Access Year-round | Tip Just outside Pooley Bridge, at the junction between Penrith and Tirrel, is an unusual fingerpost with a crown on the top. This unusual finial for a road sign is painted in bright red, white, blue and green, a jolly addition to an otherwise bland direction post.

83 St Michael's, Barton

Ancient and architecturally unique

Pooley Bridge is an attractive small town by Ullswater, but it can turn into a busy tourist centre during the peak season. For this reason, it is known locally as 'the Bowness of the North'. So it's all the more surprising that an architecturally unique church standing a stone's throw away is completely off the beaten track. St Michael's, Barton shouldn't be confused with another fabulous Norman church going by the same name in Barton-le-Street. That one is in Yorkshire.

The stunning building dates back to Norman times, the 12th century. The church was built on a site of prehistoric origins. It is approached through the graveyard via a roofed gateway, or 'lych-gate', which doubles as a war memorial for the men of Barton who died during World War I. St Michael's has a few unsettling aspects to it. For example, it is unusual for a church to stand in the centre of a circular graveyard, as this one does. Its disproportionately broad central square tower is not common either. The squat tower used to serve as a refuge for local families when the Scottish reivers (see ch. 23) rampaged through the countryside. The church's alliance to England is represented by a striking stone head which can be found in the north aisle. The face bears a strong resemblance to Edward I, known for his brutal conduct towards the Scots. It is quite remarkable that the sculpture was not desecrated as the Borders war raged.

But the most extraordinary features are the two double-chancel arches built to support the tower. This type of architecture is unique in the area. Visitors on a Wordsworth trail will love St Michael's, as a large number of the Wordsworth family is remembered here, away from the Grasmere hubbub. Grandfather Richard is buried here, and there are memorials to uncle John and his two wives, along with aunt Anne who married the curate.

Address Tirril, Penrith, CA10 2LR, https://barton-church-ullswater.uk | Getting there Clearly signposted just off B 5320 towards Pooley Bridge, 1 mile west of Tirril | Access Year-round | Tip There is a Wordsworth trail around Penrith taking in sites such as the building where William and Dorothy attended school. Its façade reflects the domestic local architecture with a porch-like gable (www.penrithtowntrails.co.uk/wordsworth.php).

84_Rannerdale Valley
Lakeland's secret valley

In all the literature written about the Lake District, the name of Rannerdale appears very seldom, so many people will have never heard it. Between Buttermere and Crummock Water lies a short but steep hill, Rannerdale Knotts, and the valley around it. They would pass almost without comment if it weren't for an event that happened a millennium ago and the bloody legend attached to it: the mighty battle of Rannerdale Knotts.

According to folklore, the invading Normans were on their way to Carlisle, advancing mercilessly. As they were doing so, Earl Jarl Boethar, who championed the northern folk, was becoming more and more troublesome with constant raids on the Norman troops. To locate his stronghold had proven very difficult until a friend of his was captured and revealed the location under torture. As the army made its way for the head of Crummock, where the Earl resided, the local spies warned him. He was then able to place his men and his Norse allies judiciously in Rannerdale. A massacre of Norman soldiers ensued. Blood covered the hills. There was so much of it that to this day the valley produces carpets of bluebells, one flower for each soldier killed. In the spring, the spectacle of the whole valley in bloom is other-worldly.

There is scope for easy ramblings but there are also many challenging hikes with the 'Buttermere Round': Red Pike, High Stile and High Crag. Wainwright loved the area, and when he died his ashes were scattered from the nearby Haystacks, his favourite mountain. Here is how he described the area in one of his pictorial guides: 'Rannerdale is seen by most visitors to Buttermere, but only as a farm and a cottage and a patchwork of fields on the shore of Crummock Water. Alongside the fields and thrusting as a headland into the lake, is the abrupt and rugged end of a low fell. This is Rannerdale Knotts, a mountain in miniature.'

Address Rannedale Valley, CA13 9UZ | **Getting there** By car, from Keswick via B 5292 or from Cockermouth by B 5289 via Lorton, free parking available at Rannerdale Knott and at Rannerdale Bridge, pay-and-display parking available in Buttermere; bus 77/77a from Keswick and 949 from Cockermouth stop in Buttermere, 1 mile away | **Access** Year-round; drive very carefully in winter | **Tip** For more on how Lakelanders engaged in long-term guerilla warfare with the Normans, try the 1930 book The Secret Valley: The Real Romance of Lakeland by Nicholas Size.

85 La'al Ratty
The Ravenglass & Eskdale Railway

In the 19th century, nothing had a more profound impact on the economy and society in the north of England than the arrival of the railways. It was a revolution. All sorts of raw materials, previously difficult to transport, could then be moved quickly from the mines to the factories. Today the mines have closed, but we still enjoy the steam railways. The Ravenglass & Eskdale Railway, affectionately known in the area by its name in old Cumbrian dialect, 'La'al Ratty', meaning Little Railway, is one of the oldest and longest narrow-gauge railways in England.

La'al Ratty opened in 1875 and carried iron ore and minerals from the local mines. Today, the seven-mile journey between Ravenglass and Dalegarth has remained the same. It takes about 40 minutes, with possibilities to alight along the way at various stops. The whole experience is a delight. Each locomotive has its own story. The green-painted River Irt is the oldest. Northern Rock was custom built. Others have been restored and returned such as Katie, a 122-year-old steam locomotive which reappeared in 2018, all bright and shiny.

You don't need to be a child to love the ride. Train drivers use a radio system, a giant walkie-talkie to communicate with the Ravenglass signal box. There are passing loops along the way. Each driver meticulously follows a 'rander board', or schedule sheet. The proven system works like clockwork leaving the passengers the time to enjoy the ever-changing scenery. No two seasons will provide the same experience. Every single member of staff, be they cashier, driver or controller, is an expert. Their love for their heritage railway is infectious. They are a very friendly bunch of people who will answer all your questions. For more information and to prolong the experience, there is a museum on site, a pub and two heritage Pullman carriages that provide holiday accommodation.

Address Ravenglass Station, CA18 1SW; Dalegarth Station, CA19 1TF,
+44 (0)1229 717171, www.ravenglass-railway.co.uk, steam@ravenglass-railway.co.uk |
Getting there By car, follow the signs for Ravenglass from A 595 turning; by rail, Northern
Rail trains between Carlisle, Whitehaven and Barrow call at Ravenglass | **Hours** La'al
Ratty operates a coloured system of timetables according to the seasons, information from
www.ravenglass-railway.co.uk/plan-visit/timetables | **Tip** If you have time, stop at Boot to
visit Eskdale Mill, still in use today, it is one of the oldest water-powered corn mills in the
Lake District.

86 Muncaster Castle Raptors
Adorable owls and mighty vultures

Come rain or shine from mid-February until 23 December, if you visit the beautiful grounds of Muncaster gardens, you'll be treated to two unmissable bird-of-prey flying displays, with Scafell Pike in the background. 'World of Owls' takes place at 11.30am, 'Sky Hunters' at 2pm. Stay a little longer and at 4pm there is an opportunity to see wild herons being fed. It's a real joy to watch Christie and Linford, two adorable burrowing owls, performing for a treat, or to observe Moriarty, an African hooded vulture, catch his food in full flight.

Innovation and adaptability have long been the strengths of Muncaster Castle and there is another important purpose to the centre. Muncaster Hawk and Owl Centre made its mission to play a role in the conservation of endangered birds, which are vital to our ecosystem. It is home to 20 kinds of birds of prey among which two are critically endangered hooded vultures.

The castle has been the residence of the Pennington family for over 800 years. Exciting archaeological digs may soon confirm that the foundations date back to the Roman era. The buildings have evolved harmoniously through the centuries to fit their times. Steeped in history, each room tells a story; the impressive medieval Great Hall with the family portraits sets the tone. But it is the clever architecture of the beautiful octagonal library that steals the show. Other rooms are said to be haunted. Catch a glimpse of the sinister portrait of the jester Tom Fool, and even the sceptics would believe the tales. In 1461, Henry VI was offered shelter by Sir John Pennington, after the Battle of Towton. He was so grateful that he offered his host a 'luck', a glass drinking bowl. It is said that as long as the vessel remains intact, the castle and its surroundings are safe from harm. Only a few members of the family know where 'The Luck of Muncaster' is kept.

Address Muncaster Castle, Ravenglass, CA18 1RQ, +44 (0)1229 717614, www.muncaster.co.uk, info@muncaster.co.uk | **Getting there** The main car park is clearly visible from A 595, while reception is 500 metres south on A 595; follow the signs for Accommodation | **Hours** Very diverse opening days and times throughout the year. Castle closed 1 Nov–23 Mar. Frequent events such as Halloween Twilight Owls or Scientific Ghost Vigil. Consult www.muncaster.co.uk/tickets. | **Tip** There are many places said to be haunted in Cumbria. Three more are in this book: Beetham (see ch. 12), Carlisle Castle (see ch. 20), The Kirkstone Pass Inn (see ch. 63).

87__Ravenglass
The last frontier

Mention the Lake District and water-words spring to mind: rivers, waterfalls, tarns… rain, the list flows on, but 'sea' is probably not on it. Out of all the National Park features, the most unexpected is a coastal village. Ravenglass has a mix of houses of various periods and styles of architecture, the main street was built with beach cobbles, and the overall effect is very attractive. Does it sound like a new tourist development? It's far from that.

It's difficult to imagine by looking at sleepy Ravenglass today that it was once a thriving port and an important naval base. Two millennia ago, it was known as Glannaventa, a key port close to the northern border of the Roman empire. It played a major role and was a lifeline for the garrisons stationed here. At some point, 500 soldiers were garrisoned at Glannaventa and thousands more relied on it for their food and essentials. Incredibly, the Roman bathhouse is still standing, and makes a fine ruin.

Though nowadays visitors don't come to Ravenglass for its Roman ruins nor do they come for its seafront. The main attraction here is La'al Ratty (see ch. 85). That said, it's worth spending time on the seafront, looking at the estuary and its three rivers. Each one is a challenge to pronounce: the Mite, the Irt and the Esk. All three have given their name to one of the miniature heritage steam engines.

Bird-spotters will love it here as well. However, birds bring a minor challenge if you have decided to picnic by the sea. Across the River Esk, there is a nature reserve, home to gulls. In the 1700, the mud flats of the estuary were put to good (though naughty) use by smugglers who landed their contraband brandy. There is no contraband involved any more, only a couple of pubs doing a roaring trade. Ravenglass may not be a typical Lake District village, but it is certainly not a place to overlook.

Address Ravenglass Roman Bath House, Walls Drive, CA18 1SF; Main Street, CA18 1SD | **Getting there** By car, the main street is a clearly indicated turn-off from A 595 between Holmrook and Muncaster. Follow the signs to the railway, where there is plenty of pay-and-display parking. By train, Ravenglass Station links with the Ravenglass & Eskdale narrow-gauge railway. | **Access** Year-round | **Tip** The village of Ravenglass shares the same cultural status as the Taj Mahal. It's one of the few places in the world to have been awarded a double World Heritage Site award.

88__ Shap Memorial
A memorial to unsung kindness

The Shap area has long been inhabited. It boasts a 12th-century ruined abbey and the highest heated swimming pool in the country. In around the 17th century there were only four roads in the whole of Cumbria and Shap was situated on one of them – the road from Kendal to Penrith. In those days, and until 1970 in fact, Shap was a very busy village. Then the northerly section of the M6 motorway opened. Shap lost its buzz, but nothing of its spirit.

The fell summit on the Kendal side is 1,397 feet above sea level. In the winter, it's not unusual for the A6 road to become snow-bound. Before the days of the M6, long lines of trucks would often get stuck. Conditions were (and still are) so dire that even special runway snow ploughs were often unable to help. On these occasions, Shap Memorial Hall provided emergency shelter, and a soup kitchen run by volunteers was set up. Villagers routinely offered lodging to stranded drivers. So, it may not come as a surprise that, on a lay-by at the summit of the A6 of Shap Fell, there is a memorial to the people who helped others to get through from Penrith to Kendal. It's a monument to grit and kindness.

The memorial was unveiled in the spring of 1994. It's a large piece of Shap pink granite. This type of rock was much used in architecture across the country, including for the bollards around St Paul's Cathedral in London. It's very distinctive, with big speckles of pink crystal, hence its name.

The Shap monument reads as follows, *This memorial pays tribute to the drivers and crews of vehicles that made possible the social and commercial links between north and south on this old and difficult route over Shap Fell before the opening of the M6 Motorway. Remembered too are those who built and maintained the road and the generations of local people who gave freely of food and shelter to stranded travellers in bad weather.*

THIS MEMORIAL PAYS TRIBUTE TO THE DRIVERS AND CREWS OF VEHICLES THAT MADE POSSIBLE THE SOCIAL AND COMMERCIAL LINKS BETWEEN NORTH AND SOUTH ON THIS OLD AND DIFFICULT ROUTE OVER SHAP FELL BEFORE THE OPENING OF THE M6 MOTORWAY.
REMEMBERED TOO ARE THOSE WHO BUILT AND MAINTAINED THE ROAD AND THE GENERATIONS OF LOCAL PEOPLE WHO GAVE FREELY OF FOOD AND SHELTER TO STRANDED TRAVELLERS IN BAD WEATHER.

Erected by the
Friends of the British Commercial Vehicle Museum
The Shap Memorial Trust Fund
with the assistance and co-operation of
Eden District Council
Cumbria County Council
Cumbria County Contracting
Shap Granite Company
Gordon Greaves, Stonemason Troutbeck Bridge

Address A6, between Shap and Kendal | Getting there The stone tribute is in a small lay-by at the top of the fell, by the southbound lane of A6, roughly 5 miles from Shap (driving towards Kendal) opposite an isolated boothy. Not a good idea to visit in bad weather. | Access Year-round, except when A6 is snowbound or icy | Tip The Old North Road between Kendal and Shap (the one used before the A6) is not difficult to spot and makes for a nice walk. Alfred Wainwright loved it and is said to have been fascinated by its history.

89__Smardale Gill Viaduct
Feats of engineering

The Smardale viaducts are definitely situated outside the Lake District National Park. In fact, they are to be found in the neighbouring park, the Yorkshire Dales.

However, the Settle–Carlisle line has played a very important role in the development of the area as a whole. During the reign of Queen Victoria, Britain was an important leader in the trading world, and expansion of the rail network was vital, but when it came to the north and its profitable mines, the dramatic geography was in the way. To get around the problem, feats of engineering were deployed, and valleys were joined by viaducts (and also aqueducts), changing the scenery for ever.

Smardale Gill Viaduct, built in 1861, is 28 metres high. Made of 14 perfect stone arches, it curves its way in an un-viaductlike fashion across the valley of Scandale Beck. The line was closed in 1962, around the time af the demise of steelmaking, but the viaduct had become a vital link to cross the valley so it was restored in 1992, and serves as a public footpath. It is not to be confused with a later viaduct, simply named Smardale Viaduct, which was made of 12 arches in local grey limestone a little farther away. It is the highest viaduct on the Settle–Carlisle Railway.

The area offers family walks with lovely views all around. The area surrounding Smardale Gill is a National Nature Reserve under the care of Cumbria Wildlife Trust. It has vibrant and rare fauna and flora, and is particularly known for its butterflies. The rarer are the Scotch Argus, which breeds only in two places in England, and the Northern Brown Argus, whose name describes its colour apart from a cream fringe around its wings and a few orange dots. May to September is the best time to see them.

This is an area for making and taking time, and an excellent place for nature photography.

Address Smardale car park, CA17 4HG | Getting there Park to the right by the bridge on the old track bed, walk a couple of minutes to the entrance of the reserve and join the path. It's a 10-minute walk to some steps on the right into Demesne Wood from where the viaduct can be seen. | Access Year-round, but walk can be muddy | Tip Audio guides for the Settle–Carlisle journey are available and describe what you can see out of the window while journeying on this iconic line (www.settle-carlisle.co.uk/tickets-times-travel/your-journey/audio-guides).

90__RSPB St Bees Head Reserve

Seabird multistorey

The red cliffs of St Bees are truly spectacular. Their colour, geologically known as St Bees New Red Sandstone, has given many Cumbrian buildings their unique dark red appearance from time immemorial. The hundred-metre drop from the cliffs can be scary, but a path safely cordons the walkers. From here, there are truly stunning views. On a clear day, the panorama stretches across the Irish Sea taking in the Isle of Man. The nature reserve situated on the headland is maintained by the Royal Society for the Protection of Birds. This is the only cliff-nesting seabird colony in the north-west of England. The cliff face is not always visible from the path but the RSPB has provided viewing platforms for bird-watching. Don't forget your binoculars.

Though there are birds all year round, from the end of March until July the cliffs come alive with over 5,000 pairs of seabirds nesting on ledges. Some are difficult to differentiate; to the untrained eye they look very much alike. It's the case for the herring gulls and the kittiwakes, which are set apart by their calls. Some species spend most of their lives at sea, like the black-and-white razorbills, landing only to breed. According to the experts, the RSPB St Bees Head Reserve hosts the most important colony of black guillemots in the north-west of England. On the cliff-top path you might spot puffins, gannets, cormorants and large black ravens. If you were very lucky, you might even witness a peregrine falcon or sparrowhawk gliding silently. Don't be too disappointed if the conditions are not quite right for such sightings; a walk along the towering cliffs to the lighthouse at the north headland and back has other charms. The flora is interesting, and the sea lavender and sea pinks may not be very easy to spot but at least they are stationary, which gives you a better chance. A day at St Bees' sandy beach is always a pleasure.

Address Beach Road, St Bees, CA27 0EN, +44 (0)1697 351330, www.rspb.org.uk/reserves-and-events/reserves-a-z/st-bees-head, stbees.head@rspb.org.uk | Getting there From St Bees village, take Beach Road, park in the shore-front car park. Access to the reserve is via the path over the metal footbridge at the north end of the promenade. St Bees station is 1 mile from the reserve; the Beach Road starts directly outside the station. | Access Year-round; best sightings during early mornings in spring | Tip St Bees beach is the start of Alfred Wainwright's 192-mile Coast to Coast walk. The beginning of the walk is marked by the 'Wainwright Wall' which retraces the route. The walk ends at the North Sea's Robin Hood's Bay.

91 St Bees Man Resting Place
Medieval knight mystery

If St Bees' oldest house is 500 years old, its oldest man is 650 years old. In 1981, St Bees Priory made the headlines when a vault containing the remains of a medieval knight was discovered. The extraordinarily well-preserved body was unearthed during an archaeological dig searching for evidence of a pre-Norman church. The knight had been tightly wrapped in a lead sheet and a pine-resin-coated shroud. The body had not been chemically embalmed, so it came as a shock to all present to discover that the man's skin was still intact, as were his beard and hair, and his inner organs. There was even liquid blood in the chest cavity. At the time, the tools to identify this person with certainty had yet to be discovered. An autopsy was performed, and he was reburied.

Visitors can follow the story in a corner of the priory dedicated to the St Bees Man with the help of the evidence such as the artefacts found in the vault and a documented photo-book. The evidence is somewhat gruesome, but the story behind it is fascinating. The grandeur of the burial vault suggests that the man had an important status, but serious detective work was required to establish his identity. In 2007, Dr Chris Knüsel, from the University of Exeter and married to Carol Palmer who had been among the cohort of students in 1981, continued the research.

The focus switched to the de Lucy family, and to the strong possibility that the body belonged to Anthony de Lucy, Lord of Cockermouth and Egremont to be precise. In 1367, he joined a few friends to assist the Teutonic Knights in the Northern Crusade in Lithuania. He didn't return alive, and many questions remain unanswered. It is hoped that DNA tests from the very few samples left will find a match. An obvious connection is to the skeleton of the St Bees Lady who was buried next to him. Could it be his sister, Lady Maud de Lucy?

Address The Priory, St Bees, CA27 0DR, +44 (0)1946 822279, www.stbeespriory.org.uk, enquiries@stbeespriory.org.uk, for guided tours: chris.robson@toysfromjunk.co.uk | Getting there St Bees is on B 5345 just south of Whitehaven. The Priory is very easy to spot as it's the tallest building near the railway station; 21 trains a day stop at St Bees, but other public transport is very sparse. | Hours Daily 9am – 5pm, please respect church services | Tip Wainwright's first televised Coast to Coast walk started from St Bees beach, just down Beach Road from the priory.

The plate armour shows that the date of this effigy is about 1370. Surprisingly this knight it shown to be holding what looks like a chalice. As only an effigy of a priest would be shown holding a chalice, it is now thought that this is an artist's error. It is very likely that this is the effigy of Anthony de Lucy (probably St. Bees Man) who was the last Lord of Cockermouth. He died abroad in 1368 and was reputed in the 18th century to be buried here.

92 Hawkshead Brewery

So, that's how they use all this water!

The Lake District has over a dozen microbreweries, giving it the highest concentration of small breweries anywhere in Britain. Most craft breweries have a tap room that provides not only freshly brewed beer but also serves as a dynamic social hub. Some small independent breweries trade only locally, some have a wider remit. A few are tiny, like Tarn Hows, located in its eponymous area, which produces around four barrels a week. Others produce weird and wonderful brews, such as Fell Brewery located in Flookburgh. Each brewery is different, and each is worth including in an itinerary whether you live in Lakeland or are visiting.

Hawkshead Brewery is best known for its hospitality – besides its beer. It was founded in 2002, in the unspoiled village of Hawkshead, sometimes referred to as 'the prettiest village in the Lake District'. The brewery relocated in 2006 to the Mill Yard beside the River Kent in Staveley. Their brewers are hands-on, the process is manual, and they are determined to keep it that way at this plant. On their new site on the western coast, however, state-of-the-art, fully automated, much faster equipment allows the brewery to meet the demand.

The first beer Hawkshead Brewery produced, in their old barn back in Hawkshead, was a bitter, quickly followed by a core range of all the real ale classics. Their market leader is the Windermere Pale brewed with Maris Otter malted barley, three traditional English hops and Citra hops. Their bestseller often sells before it finishes brewing. But not every beer has a traditional taste, and the brewery adapts to the trends. Their sour beers are full of surprises, such as Tonka, a brew delicately flavoured with tonka beans, and Tiramisu, a milk stout brewed with coffee beans roasted locally. The Hawkshead brewers are certainly kept busy, innovating new beers and consolidating their core offer.

Address Staveley, Kendal, LA8 9LR, +44 (0)1539 822644, www.hawksheadbrewery.co.uk, info@hawksheadbrewery.co.uk | Getting there Halfway between Kendal and Windermere, off A591. Follow signs for Staveley, where there are brown tourist signs for the brewery, off Back Lane. Staveley is on the regular 555/554 bus route from Lancaster or Keswick and is served by trains on the Windermere-Oxenholme line. | Hours Daily tours at 1pm; call ahead to book your place | Tip The CAMRA Westmorland branch website is very useful to keep up with local news and it publishes a very popular overground Cumbria breweries poster (www.westmorland.camra.org.uk).

93__Tarn Hows

Mirror, mirror, which is the fairest of them all?

If you were asked to draw a picture of an idyllic tarn (small mountain lake), you might come up with something closely resembling Tarn Hows. Situated between the villages of Coniston and Hawkshead, it has often been described as the perfect tarn. Tarn Hows is man-made, which explains its beautiful proportions. Originally, it was three small tarns, rather unimaginatively called High Tarn, Low Tarn and Middle Tarn. Until 1862, the area was a part of the open common grazing of Hawshead parish. In his guidebook to the Lakes, Wordsworth mentions the area but doesn't pay any heed to the tarns. It didn't get much better 50 years later when another writer, G. D. Abraham, described Tarn Hows simply as, 'Set wildly among larches and heather slopes.'

Much has changed since then thanks to James Marshall, Member of Parliament for Leeds and owner of the land, who embarked on a series of landscape improvements. The surroundings, footpaths and picnic areas were carefully designed for maximum impact. The woodland plantations were expanded. Spruce, larch and pine trees were planted around the tarn. When in 1930 the Marshall family sold 4,000 acres to Beatrix Potter for £15,000, it was already a famous beauty spot. She, in turn, sold half to the National Trust, which is still managing it to this day, and bequeathed them the other half.

Tarn Hows is at its best on a bright clear day when the Langdale Pikes to the north and the mighty Helvellyn make for a dramatic background. The surface of the lake is like a blue mirror and reflects the mountains. Keep an eye out for red squirrels and, between March and October – the ice-cream van! The 1.5-mile, pushchair- and wheelchair-friendly path around the tarn makes for a nice family walk. Though it can be packed with people walking and picnicking in the summer, its unique charm means it's not to be missed.

Address Tarn Hows, LA21 8DP | **Getting there** From B 5285 turn onto the minor road running between Hawkshead and Coniston. Tarn Hows is 1 mile from the junction and clearly indicated, with a large National Trust car park. Bus 505 operates between Coniston and Hawkshead, stopping at Hawkshead Hill, a roughly 1-mile walk away, generally uphill. The tarn can be reached on foot from either Hawkshead (1.5 miles) or Coniston (2.1 miles), one of the loveliest parts of the Cumbrian Way. | **Access** Year-round | **Tip** There is plenty to do around Tarn Hows. Perhaps take a cruise in the beautiful steam yacht Gondola on Coniston Water and hear all about the area (www.nationaltrust.org.uk/steam-yacht-gondola).

94___ Red River

A beautiful seat

To mark the new millennium, the East Cumbria Countryside Project commissioned a series of stone sculptures to be placed by public footpaths along the River Eden. It's one of the few large rivers in England that flows northwards. The river traverses the Vale of Eden, which is an ancient rift basin between the Lake District and the North Pennines.

The project's brief was for 10 different artists to create 10 site-specific carved stone sculptures that would function as seats, with the aim to explore peoples' emotional reactions to the landscape. The sculptures, located at intervals along the 70 miles of river, encourage the public to stop, sit and ponder the beautiful river, its environment, its ecology and our impact on it. The first of them, *Water Cut*, is situated at the source of the Eden, high up in Mallerstang Common. Created by Mary Bourne, it is a block of limestone split in two by the shape of a meandering river – a striking piece to kick off *The Eden Benchmarks* series.

Closer to the Lake District, there is Victoria Bransford's *Red River*, a sandstone sculpture situated north of the village of Temple Sowerby. The artist's work often relates to ecology. This block of carved sandstone topped with perfect spheres lies on the ground. Its shape recalls the curves of the river below. Flowing curves are carved on the top to represent the water it overlooks. The spheres are static, but when you first look at them it seems that these giant pebbles could be carried away by the energy of the stone water and tumble in the river below. The stones reflect the same light and shade at the same time, in perfect harmony, though this trick of light is more obvious in photographs than in real life. At the end of the trail at Rockcliffe, where the river reaches the sea, sits *Global Warming* by Kenyan-born artist Antony Turner, which resembles planet Earth carefully held in a hand.

Address Temple Sowerby, CA10 1RZ, www.edenbenchmarks.org.uk | Getting there Temple Sowerby is situated on B 6412 near A 66, 8 miles east of Penrith. From the north end of the village follow the public footpath, clearly signposted, alongside the cricket ground, bearing right diagonally across to the far corner of the field and then sharp right, over the stile. | Access Year-round | Tip Temple Sowerby has been known as the 'Queen of Westmorland Villages' for several hundred years, for its beautiful buildings and houses. The use of 'Temple' comes from the Knights Templar who once held the manor. There has been a maypole in the village for at least two centuries.

95 Thirlmere

May the water be with you

Thirlmere isn't exactly what it appears to be. It looks like a lake but is in reality a valley that was flooded to become Lakeland's first reservoir. At the end of the 19th century, Manchester had developed fast and the need for water had increased exponentially. Water was required to power its mills, factories and its large population of workers.

The solution lay in the sparsely populated Thirlmere valley. Not everyone was happy with the proposal to create the reservoir here, and a strong opposition was mounted, led by John Ruskin, but the campaign was unsuccessful, and the valley duly flooded. The villages of Wythburn and Armboth, along with countless farms, were submerged. It may have looked strange at the time, but modern visitors are hard pressed to spot the difference between this reservoir and a natural lake.

What was deemed a natural disaster has had its benefits. Thirlmere contains 11 per cent of the north-west's water supply. Every now and then, around the reservoir, there is a reminder of Thirlmere's function. On the east shore stands what looks just like a castle with battlements and a coat of arms, but is in fact a straining well for filtration. The valve housed inside controls the water supplied to major towns and cities in Lancashire and Greater Manchester. The first water was transported to Manchester on 12 October, 1894. It took 27 hours to reach its goal.

In 2014, it was briefly relocated to the planet Takodana for *Star Wars: The Force Awakens*. Despite the location details being kept under wraps, a Manchester photographer recognised Thirlmere. Recently there was talk of stringing eight zip wires up for visitors to fly across the reservoir. A campaign was mounted, yet again, led this time by several conservationist groups. It was a more successful campaign than the original reservoir protest, and the project was dropped.

Address Thirlmere, CA12 4TN | Getting there 10 minutes by car from Grasmere. There are several car parks around the reservoir, each has comprehensive information panels. The closest to the straining well is at Wythburn Church. All buses along A 591 between Grasmere and Keswick stop on the east shore at Wythburn, the King's Head and Thirlspot. | Access Year-round | Tip Wythburn Church, by the A 591 on the east bank of Thirlmere, is an isolated little church, a favourite of the Romantic poets.

96_ Burne-Jones' Vitrail

Artist's vision for all to admire in Troutbeck

In the latter part of the 19th century, artist and designer Edward Burne-Jones had become famous for his work, which can now be seen in the Birmingham Museum and Art Gallery and other major museums. When he was still at university, he formed a friendship with William Morris that lead him to employment in Powell's Glass Works. Along with Rossetti, one his fellow artists, they became members of the original Pre-Raphaelite Brotherhood. A little later, when William Morris formed a furnishings and decorative arts manufacturer, nicknamed 'The Firm', Burne-Jones became its major stained-glass window designer. His romantic medieval-inspired shapes and lavish palette of colours are unmistakable.

The Firm created all kinds of beautiful art from murals to furniture. One of their main activities was church decoration. This is how the small Jesus Church, in the charming hamlet of Troutbeck near Windermere (not to be confused with the village of the same name near Penrith), acquired its stunning stained-glass panels for its east window.

The panels were made in the workshops of Morris & Co. Morris himself designed the greenery and the window was worked on by three major Pre-Raphaelite artists – Burne-Jones, Ford Madox Brown and Morris. The window is particularly large for the size of the church. The entire wall is filled with scenes from the Bible, from Jesus blessing children to the Last Supper. Greens are the dominant colours, complemented by reds, golds and an array of blues. All the characters are striking for their humanity. The Crucifixion panel in the centre is flanked by two others representing Mary and John. The main panel is slightly anachronistic as Jesus on the cross doesn't have a beard. The current church dates back to 1736. The seats are simple oak benches and quite modern. Notice the nice cross-stitched cushions depicting country scenes.

Address Troutbeck, LA23 1PB, +44 (0)1539 443032, www.troutbeck.org/ jesus_church_about_us.html | **Getting there** From Windermere follow A 591 west to A 592. Follow A 592 for 3 miles, and Jesus Church will become visible after you cross a stone bridge. Windermere train and bus stations are just over an hour's uphill walk away. Follow Orrest Head path until you see a sign for A 592 Troutbeck Road. | **Hours** Daily 9am – dusk | **Tip** There are more examples of stained-glass windows designed by Burne-Jones and made by Morris & Co in Cumbria. Some are well known, such as the amazing panels of St Martin's in Brampton. Worth including on an itinerary are St Paul's in Irton and Christ & St Mary in Armathwaite.

97 Aira Force

Feel the force

There are very few outdoor attractions that get better when the weather is wetter, but this is the case for waterfalls, of which there are many in Lakeland. If you have time to visit only one, choose Aira Force near the village of Watermillock. At 20 metres high and composed of several cascades, Aira Force ranks fourth highest in England. A bridge at the top and another at the bottom act as viewing platforms.

There are several ways to get to the majestic spectacle. You can join the many visitors who start their ascent from the National Trust car park. This way you'll get the benefit of the neatly designed walking trails, which were part of a pleasure garden in the 1770s. The trails take in a fascinating collection of trees, all neatly recorded, including two money trees similar to that of the Coffin Trail (see ch. 41) by Dove Cottage. Or park near the village of Dockray and follow the stream, Aira Beck, down. This way you'll get good views of Ullswater in the distance and the opportunity to walk through ancient woodlands. However, this route is not neatly signposted. There is a third way, which is to use the National Trust car park, making sure that you schedule your visit in the early morning or late afternoon in order to avoid the crowds. Whichever solution you choose, to witness the Aira Force cascading down is an awesome spectacle. You might even get lucky enough to take a picture of a rainbow over the water.

Aira Force is on the western side of Gowbarrow Fell, the summit of which is at 481 metres. It was while visiting the hillside of Gowbarrow in the spring of 1802 that Dorothy Wordsworth made a mention of the famous daffodils in her diary. Two years later, William Wordsworth wrote his famous 'Daffodils' poem, borrowing his sister's exact words. He also immortalised Lady Emma, the beautiful ghost of the Force in his poem, 'The Somnambulist'.

Address Aira Force, CA11 0JS, +44 (0)1768 482067, www.nationaltrust.org.uk/aira-force-and-ullswater, ulsswater@nationaltrust.org.uk | **Getting there** By boat with the Ullswater Steamers from Glenridding or Pooley Bridge; by car, from A 66 take A 5091, the paths to and from the car park can comfortably be done within 40 minutes; bus 508, the Kirkstone Rambler, runs from Penrith to Windermere over the Kirkstone Pass; there is a train from Penrith to Patterdale | **Access** Year-round | **Tip** The highest waterfall in the Lake District is Scale Force, a 2.5-mile walk from Buttermere car park.

98 Hoad Monument

Ulverston's pepper pot

What is a lighthouse doing on the top of a hill, one mile away from the sea? The answer is simple: this iconic symbol known locally as 'Hoad' or 'the pepper pot' was never built as a beacon for navigation. To confuse things further, the volunteers who man the monument, flying a flag on the hill when the tower is open, are called 'lighthouse keepers'.

The 30.5-metre tower at the top of Hoad Hill, built in 1850 by public subscription, is in fact a memorial to Sir John Barrow. Its real name is The Sir John Barrow Monument. The tower underwent a £1.1-million restoration in 2009 – 10. Inside the tower, there is a narrow spiral staircase of 112 steps leading to the lantern chamber. The windows offer a glorious 360-degree panorama over Morecambe Bay, the Langdales and the Yorkshire Dales. The walk to the monument from Ulverston is a little bit taxing but the views are well worth the effort.

Sir John Barrow was born in Ulverston (now an attractive town with plenty of traditional shops) in 1764. Son of a local tanner, his career was extraordinary. Excelling in maths, he left the local school at the age of 13. Soon he was teaching the subject at a school in Greenwich before starting on his first expedition to China in 1792. As an explorer and First Sea Lord, he helped discover Antarctica. Historian Fergus Fleming describes what happened in his book *Barrow's Boys*: 'For 30 years beginning in 1816, the British Admiralty's John Barrow and his elite team charted large areas of the Arctic, discovered the North Magnetic Pole, were the first to see volcanoes in the Antarctic, crossed the Sahara to find Timbuktu and the mouth of the Niger.' Sir John Barrow was also a founder member of the Royal Geographical Society. He died in 1848, aged 84. It was his great-great-great-grandson, the 7th Baronet of Ulverston, who re-opened the monument in 2010.

Address Ulverston, LA12 7LD | **Getting there** Access to the monument is on foot only from the town centre. Two well-indicated routes start in Ford Park and Chittery Lane. Parking available in Ulverston town centre and Ford Park. | **Hours** Sun, from Easter to Oct; walk: year-round, weather permitting | **Tip** The nearest real lighthouse is located on Walney Island in Barrow-in-Furness.

99 Kadampa Buddhist Temple

A Buddhist world peace temple open to everyone

A couple of miles outside Ulverston, past the modern suburban development, along the A 5087 and down a country road stands the historic Conishead Priory. It was built in the 12th century, as a hospital for the poor. Subsequently, this Augustinian Priory, like the phoenix, rose from its ashes, many a time. This important landmark, with its striking Victorian Gothic frontage, flanked by two 30-metre octagonal towers, has had many functions. Since their first life as a priory, the buildings have been a private house, a hydropathic hotel, a military hospital and a miners' convalescent home, before changing hands once more in 1976. By then, the house, which was in a terrible state of disrepair and on the verge of collapse, and the grounds, were bought by Manjushri Kadampa Meditation Centre.

No expense was spared. More than £1 million was invested to carefully restore this historic treasure. Though more needs to be done, the buildings are now safe and look splendid once again. The grounds are beautiful too. Gardens and a woodland lead gently to a beach on the shores of Morecambe Bay. But the most incredible vision, in this part of the world, is the Kadampa World Peace Temple. It's an attractive place with a special architecture designed by Venerable Geshe Kelsang Gyatso and features the largest bronze Buddha statue in the West. A board at the gate explains the basic architectural principles: the temple has four doorways symbolizing the four ways to enter the path to liberation. Above each doorway, there is a golden representation of a male and female deer with the Dharma Wheel. A golden, five-pronged Vajra symbolizing the completion of the spiritual path sits at the very top of the temple roof. Above the colonnades are the eight auspicious symbols showing how to progress along the spiritual path. It's an uplifting experience in an unexpected location.

Address Manjushri Kadampa Meditation Center, Conishead Priory, Ulverston, LA12 9QQ, +44 (0)1229 584029, https://manjushri.org, info@manjushri.org | **Getting there** 45-minute walk from Ulverston; bus 11 from Ulverston library. By car, from Ulverston take A 5087 coast road for Bardsea / Croftlands and 'Coastal route to Barrow'. After 2 miles look for the brown and white tourist sign. Parking on site. | **Hours** Mon – Sat 11am – 5pm, Sun noon – 5pm; daily 15-minute guided meditation at 12.30pm & 2pm | **Tip** In the grounds of the Priory, the World Peace Café in a sunny conservatory serves vegan, vegetarian and gluten-free food.

100_ Laurel & Hardy Museum

A comedy of errors

Stan Laurel is today Ulverston's most famous son, but it hasn't always been the case. For over half a century, it was thought that Laurel was born in either Bishop Auckland or North Shields, where his parents, Arthur and Margaret Jefferson, were respectively theatre owner and actress. It took Bill Cubin, a devotee of Laurel and Hardy, much perseverance to prove that Arthur Stanley Jefferson was born in his grandparents' house in Argyll Street, Ulverston, in June 1890. It must have been a proud moment for Bill Cubin, when in the early 70s, he found Laurel's birth certificate. Once it was established that the small town could claim Laurel, much happened in his honour. There is a bronze statue of Laurel and Hardy leaning on a lamp post in front of the Coronation Hall, and a three-metre-high Laurel mural created in 2014 by a local artist decorates a wall of the museum.

The museum itself is hosted in the former Roxy cinema, run nowadays by Bill Cubin's oldest grandson Mark. It is an Ali Baba cavern filled with memorabilia and touching tributes to the comedian. Visitors can follow Laurel's life on and off the screen. Look for a 1910 photo of a troupe of actors on a voyage to the US. See if you can spot fresh-faced Laurel with Chaplin. This amazing range of memorabilia is the largest such collection in the world. It even includes Laurel's grandparents' furniture. There is also a mini old-fashioned cinema where visitors can watch the duo's black-and-white short comedies or attend special screenings. Laurel was the duo's genius scriptwriter, but he always made sure that Hardy got equal billing. Though he lived in the States all his life, Laurel stayed fond of Ulverston. The reverse was also true: on their British tour in 1953, thousands of people lined the streets. It is said that the duo had absolutely no idea they were so famous.

Address The Roxy, Brogden Street, Ulverston, +44 (0)1229 582292, www.laurel-and-hardy.co.uk, info@laurel-and-hardy.co.uk | **Getting there** Ulverston has a train and coach station; there is a pay-and-display car park near the museum. | **Hours** Easter–Oct, daily 10am–5pm; closed Mon & Wed the rest of the year | **Tip** If you love black-and-white films, stop at Carnforth railway station for 'a brief encounter'. The 1945 love story was filmed in the café.

101__ Start of the Cumbrian Way

Sit on a compass bench or a squirrel bench

From April to October, it's possible to walk the 119km Cumbrian Way, which cuts through the Lake District National Park from south to north, starting at the market town of Ulverston and finishing in the city of Carlisle, or vice versa. The start of the Cumbrian Way in Ulverston is marked by a sculpture of a compass with a cairn of rocks in its centre. The rocks are representative of the area's geology, which is shown on the side of the cairn together with an Ordnance Survey map referencing key points along the route. The sculpture was installed in February 2002 and is the work of sculptor Chris Brammall, whose studio sits at the edge of the Lake District National Park.

If this impressive multimedia piece of art is striking, it's got competition in an iconic, colourful, cast-iron 'squirrel bench' by the stone bridge over the Gill. The metal squirrel seats were originally donated by GlaxoSmithKline on the 50th anniversary of the company. There are 50 such benches dotted around Ulverston. These public seats are slatted wooden seats with sides decorated with the Furness Railway's bench design, a cast-iron bushy-tailed red squirrel munching on a purple bunch of grapes, hanging from a blue vine. The long, slender stem of each metal plant creeps and trails, winding itself up and down to form the metal sides of the benches.

The Cumbrian Way was developed in the 1970s. This popular walk takes in the natural beauty of the Lake District. While it is a low-level walk, the route has significant inclines and a rugged terrain requiring a certain level of fitness. Along the way, the tarns and boggy areas provide a habitat for carnivorous plants including sundew and butterwort. Crossing woodlands, there might be opportunities to spot a few real red squirrels; however, it's a much safer bet to take a few pictures of the 'squirrel bench' at the start of the hike.

Address At the far end of The Gill car park, Unnamed Road, Ulverston, LA12 7BN |
Getting there The Gill car park is situated west of Ulverston. Take Stanley Street until
you can go no further; the car park is on your right. | **Access** Year-round | **Tip** To see more
examples of Victorian wrought iron, head east along the A590 to Grange-over-Sands
station where the metalwork has been restored to its former glory.

102 Ulverston Canal

The straightest, the widest, the deepest of them all

The Lakes area has a long tradition of unique transport proposals, and the Ulverston Canal completed in 1796 is no different. Its description alone sounds very much like a pub quiz question: the Ulverston Canal is claimed to be the deepest (4.6m), the widest (20m) and the straightest canal in the UK. It isn't the shortest, but at just over 1 mile, it isn't far off. Due to its difficult terrain, Cumbria doesn't have many canals; in fact, there are only three.

In the early 1700s, Ulverston was a busy trading town, and coal and iron were transported to and from the sea at Morecambe Sands. In the midst of 'canal mania', local solicitor William Burnthwaite led a town meeting where it was decided to build a canal to cut costs. And with that, Ulverston became a port. The port status had the added advantage of cutting shipping taxes, and as a result Ulverston grew even more buoyant, doubling its population. The Ulverston Canal was also used by steamers bound for Liverpool and passenger ships to London and Scotland. The gains were short-lived, however, as in 1851 the Furness Railway Company opened a railway line. The canal was used for the last time in 1916, and fell into disuse after World War I.

Today, walking the length of the canal from Ulverston to the sea is a pleasant, flat walk taking 2.5 hours at most along good pathways. A rare rolling bridge designed to retract on wheels into a small dock built into the south bank, a viaduct, an old quarry and rich fauna including geese, ducks and herons can be seen. It's still very industrial, though.

The canal runs alongside the sprawling KlaxonSmithKline pharmaceutical complex, once the owner of this waterway and still helping with its upkeep when the need arises. The seaside at the end of the walk is especially pretty at sunset. There is an inn for weary (or not) walkers and a lock-keeper's cottage.

Address Ulverston off A 590, the entrance lies on the south side of the road, between two bus stops, one on either side | Getting there 15-minute walk from the 'cairn and compass'. By car, take A 590 (Canal Road) east out of town. The entry is on the right after North Londsdale Road, opposite a bus stop, difficult to spot as you travel a busy road. Pull into the signposted turning for the canal and then turn sharp right inside to park. | Access Year-round | Tip The Lake District has a large number of remnants from its industrial past, including Elizabethan salt pans south of Allonby.

103__RB Woodall

Cumberland sausages don't fear the Wurst

Something delicious has been happening for nearly 200 years at the western edge of Lakeland, in the hamlet of Waberthwaite. Something which has not passed unnoticed, and was even spotted by the Duke of Edinburgh. As HRH Prince Philip visited a trade fair in Penrith, he tasted Woodall's products. So smitten by their Cumberland sausages was he that the royal household bestowed them the highest seal of approval: a royal warrant, originally for sausages, now for bacon. The plaque marking the event is proudly displayed on the frontage of the shop-cum-post office, which doesn't appear to have altered much since Victorian times. Like many ventures in these parts of the country, it all started back in the 1800s, with an impoverished widow in need of extra income. When her husband died, Mrs Hannah Woodall began curing meat using local pigs, salt, sugar and saltpetre. The business still operates on the same principles, run now by the seventh, eighth and ninth generations of the Woodall family.

Some speculate that Cumberland sausage originated with German miners who came to Cumbria in the 1500s to work. While most pork bangers on the market are made with 60% meat, it may come as a surprise that RB Woodall's Cumberland sausages contain 98% pork shoulder and belly. Of course, everything is down to the spicing – pepper, mace and nutmeg enter in the composition, but the rest is a trade secret. The Woodalls are tight-lipped about the exact mixture. They are only prepared to reveal that the secret is kept by one member of the family at any time. There is one thing we know for certain: a Cumberland sausage is a continuous coil. At RB Woodall, coils in the main weigh 500g each. Cumberland sausages can be as long as the natural skin allows. RB Woodall goods are sold on the premises, delivered locally or by mail order and can't be found in supermarkets.

Address Lane End, Waberthwaite, near Millom, LA19 5YJ, +44 (0)1229 717237 or +44 (0)1229 717386, www.rbwoodall.co.uk, mail@rbwoodall.com | Getting there Waberthwaite is 2 miles south-east of Ravenglass. By car, from A 595 enter the hamlet of Waberthwaite, turn down past the school, the shop is on the right. | Hours Mon–Fri 8.30am–12:45pm & 1.15–5pm, Sat 8.30am–noon | Tip Cumberland food, unlike any other regional food in England, is spicy. This is because in the 18th century, all sorts of tropical spices landed in Whitehaven (see ch. 39 for Grasmere Gingerbread).

104_ St Olaf's Church
Small but perfectly formed

This isolated little church located in a grove of evergreens, at the very end of Wasdale Road, demonstrates perfectly that churches don't have to be lavishly ornate to be beautiful. St Olaf's with its mossy slate roof and dark grey walls will lift the visitors' spirits even before they push the heavy wooden door to contemplate the chapel's interior. The tiny building, fit for 50 worshippers, looks even smaller than it really is because of the mighty fells that overshadow it. St Olaf's Church can be described with many superlatives: it's the smallest church in England near the deepest lake and highest mountain. Prior to 1977, the church may have needed them all, as it had no name. Reverend Raymond Bowers suggested St Olaf as a patronym. All the connections were in place for this fitting name. Though the church records go back to 1550 only, it's thought that there was a church on this site long before then. It's also said that the four roof trusses came from a Viking longship. Olaf II Haraldsson was king of Norway from 1015 to 1028; he greatly increased the acceptance of Christianity in Norway, and was canonised a year after his death.

With the close presence of the mighty Scafell Pike and the other surrounding mountain ranges, St Olaf's is closely associated with the local and international mountaineering community. Wasdale Head itself is referred to as the birthplace of mountaineering. Inside the church, there is a glass pane with a picture of the Nape Needle dedicated to the members of the Fell and Rock Climbing Club who died in World War I. Next to the church, the small cemetery with the graves and memorials of those killed while rock climbing is another sober reminder of the dangers of mountaineering. On a happier note, after all the exertion, climbers of all abilities have found comfort in the home of rock climbing: The Inn, previously known as the Wasdale Head Inn.

Address Wasdale Head, CA20 1EX | Getting there There is only one road into Wasdale Head, through Nether Wasdale village. Proceeding north-east from Nether Wasdale, the road splits. The right fork runs alongside Wastwater, the left fork takes you up onto the hillside but joins the lower lake road approximately halfway to Wasdale Head. The road is one lane wide with passing places and busy traffic in both directions. | Hours Open during daytime; services on Christmas Day and Easter Sunday and most Sundays during summer | Tip If you are interested in the Norse and Viking heritage of the area, make sure you visit Gosforth Cross (see ch. 37).

105 Wastwater

The deepest, the highest, the smallest

Wastwater has it all. It's the deepest lake in England at 79 metres deep, with its bottom below sea level. At the Wasdale Head end, visitors will find St Olaf, the smallest church in England (see ch. 104). In the background are the highest mountain ranges in the country including Great Gable and Scafell. So now you have Wastwater's facts file, but nothing prepares the visitor for its exceptional beauty. It's a Lakeland classic, containing all the elements we think of when we think of the Lake District – so much so that its outline forms the basis for the National Park's logo. The Wastwater Screes, just 'the Screes' for short, draw a huge, nearly vertical curtain of loose volcanic rocks across the slopes on the east side of the lake, the result of erosion. Their anthracite colour gives the dales their dark and mysterious atmosphere. When the unstable screes crumble and plunge down into the lake, the smooth dark water bubbles and spits in response.

Mysterious in other ways, Wastwater also has a ghost, the Wasdale Lady. In autumn 1976, Margaret Hogg was strangled by her husband. He drove her body all the way up from Surrey, at the other end of the country. On arrival, he rowed an inflatable boat to the middle of the lake and dumped the body there, weighted with concrete. It was only in 1984, during a search for the body of a missing French student, that the remains of Mrs Hogg were found. Due to the lack of oxygen, her body had not decomposed. Margaret Hogg was not the only strange discovery found at the bottom of the lake. In 2005, a gnome garden complete with picket fences was removed by the police. It had been luring divers for too long, causing casualties.

It's possible to canoe or row on the lake but you'll require a permit, which can be obtained from the National Trust office situated at Wasdale Head Camping. Something Mr Hogg probably omitted to do.

Address Wasdale Head, CA20 1EX | Getting there Approach by a single-track road from A 595 at Gosforth or Santon Bridge. The drive up (or down) is an experience, so take it easy and use lay-bys to allow oncoming vehicles to pass. The road terminates at Wasdale Head. The nearest main rail station is Seascale (near Gosforth), about 30 minutes away by car. | Access Year-round, but dangerous in bad weather | Tip To add to its superlatives, Wasdale is also known for the biggest liar in the world. A 19th-century local inn owner used to tell very tall tales, and an annual competition is held in his honour. Politicians and lawyers are excluded as they are considered professionals.

106_ Whinlatter Forest
Putting the mountain in mountain biking

Whinlatter Forest, situated in the North Lakes near Keswick, like Grizedale Forest near Hawkshead in the South Lakes (see ch. 46), is very popular with a wide variety of visitors. It offers an array of outdoor activities. Many visitors come because the forest is home to the longest purpose-built mountain bike trails in the Lake District.

All the trails are colour coded, like the Altura trail, which is composed of 11 miles of red route, and is mostly a narrow single track, very bumpy-looking to the untrained eye. All the routes have challenges along the way, obstacles to wiggle around or over, as the case may be. There are many cycling trails around the country but few offer an experience in such beautiful forest with arresting views. When the first cycle tracks appeared, the local population was not very pleased about this new development. Groups closely monitored the access to the forest and the potential impact on the local environment. The main argument was that nature was providing its own tracks and anything else was superfluous. As time went by, it has been proven that the centre attracts families as well as individuals to an area which otherwise may not have been very popular. In spite of all its beauty, the forest competes with many other natural sites which are more accessible.

If you are not a skilled mountain biker but still like cycling, Whinlatter Forest offers less difficult routes. In fact, there is something for everyone with or without a bicycle. Some trails are specifically designed for children. WildPlay trail, for example, has nine different play zones to explore the forest and learn basic engineering skills. The walking trails may provide encounters with the local wildlife; red squirrels like it here. For an (almost) assured osprey sighting in season, the visitor centre has a live camera feed to the nest situated in the valley below Dodd Wood (see ch. 60).

Address Braithwaite, CA12 5TW | Getting there From Keswick, take the A66 towards Cockermouth, turn left at Braithwaite onto the B5292 to Lorton; from Cockermouth take B5292 over the Whinlatter Pass; paid parking on site. Stagecoach bus 77 goes through Whinlatter. | Hours Daily 10am–4pm; cycle shop and café open till 5pm; car park and trails dawn–dusk | Tip Besides Dodd Wood (see ch. 60) and Grizedale Forest (see ch. 46) you can also visit Ennerdale Forest. The walks and trails are rarely busy.

107 Whinlatter Pass
In it to win it

The Whinlatter Pass is a mountain pass at an elevation of 318 metres above sea level. It's located on the scenic route between Keswick and Cockermouth known as the B 5292 road. The climb starts in the village of Braithwaite, two miles west of Keswick, or at High Lorton on the Cockermouth side. The road takes in three passes along the way, and the scenery is outstanding. There are parking spaces dotted here and there, some landscaped with benches to take in the views of Lake Bassenthwaite 10 miles away. Even at such a distance, the lake is clearly visible.

The B 5292 is a mountain road and must be driven with caution. It's wise to check the weather before undertaking the drive, especially during the winter. However, it's far less difficult to climb than its local counterparts. It was classified as the easiest and the most accessible of the six big lake passes. The top is marked by the entry sign to Whinlatter Forest (see ch. 106). The pass is one of the features in the Fred Whitton Challenge, the most popular cycle race in Cumbria. This road is a favourite with cyclists; though hard going, it has the big advantage of being a steady climb rather than a steep up-and-down affair. The average gradient is 7 per cent with a maximum of 15 per cent.

In 2016, this pass was the second stage in the Tour of Britain cycle race. This was the portion of the road that determined the first King of the Mountains. It's unlikely that the Tour's cyclists had time to put a foot down to admire the scenery as they approached the top, but they can't have missed noticing the Skiddaw Massif. The mountain directly opposite the pass is often referred to as 'Misty Skiddaw'. It gets its nickname from the fact that its top is often hidden in the clouds. If you are waiting for a photo opportunity, don't despair, the views change very quickly, and sometimes it clears up in less than five minutes.

Address On B 5292 between Lorton and Braithwaite | Getting there By car, take A 66 to Braithwaite and drive 2 miles along B 5292; bus 77 is a loop from Keswick to Keswick stopping at Whinlatter Visitor Centre on the pass | Access Year-round, often covered in snow in winter and sometimes closed due to accidents. Check traffic warnings. | Tip On the way from Lorton to Whinlatter Visitor Centre, there is a car park from where you can take a short walk to the Spout Force waterfall.

108_ Rum Story
Lock, stock and barrel

Whitehaven was a tiny fishing village in the 17th century. A hundred years later, it had become one of the busiest English ports, rivalling Liverpool and Bristol. Savvy local business entrepreneurs, such as the Lowthers (see ch. 77) and the Jeffersons accumulated great wealth. But the town experienced a reversal of fortune. Nowadays, the centre with its Georgian town houses looks a little worse for wear while a multimillion-pound regeneration scheme has transformed the harbour.

The historic role of Whitehaven was not forgotten in the redevelopment plans. One of the flagship attractions of the Millennium Project was The Rum Story. The museum is located in the original 1785 premises of the Jefferson family business. The Jeffersons traded in wines from Spain and Portugal and rum, sugar and molasses from the West Indies. Visitors to The Rum Story enter the museum through the Jefferson Clerk Office. The room has been left exactly how it was found. From this room, an empire was built and rum played a role in its history.

As visitors follow the signage, they slowly uncover the story of the rum creation and trade via little tableaux. It starts in the Antiguan rainforest, complete with sound effects – you'll be glad to know that the leeches are long gone. Then comes a sugar factory manned by slaves. English gentry and traders made a fortune in the transatlantic slave trade. Goods from Europe and the New World were shipped to Africa, sold in return for slaves who then were transported to the New World. The museum doesn't shy away from the dark side of the past; rum fuelling crime, drunkenness and slavery are clearly depicted. The tour tells many stories such as the link between rum and the navy, rum and *Titanic*, you'll learn why grog was invented and how Nelson was pickled in a barrel of his favourite brandy after his death. The exhibition ends with the US Prohibition.

Address Lowter Street, Whitehaven, CA28 7DN, +44 (0)1946 592933, www.rumstory.co.uk, info@rumstory.co.uk | Getting there 5-minute walk from the harbour. There are several well-indicated pay-and-display car parks dotted around the centre. | Hours Daily 10am–4.30pm, last admission 3.30pm | Tip To get practical information and a pocket guide on Whitehaven, download the app from www.whitehavenappsolutely.co.uk.

109 Lakeland – the Store

A Lake District success story

Lakeland, the home-shopping pioneers, has a special place in the heart of the nation. It has been going strong for over half a century without fighting unnecessary wars with its competitors. From the beginning, this family firm focused on its customers' needs, a principle reflected in their Windermere flagship store. The modernist glass building with its easy-to-navigate shop, natural light and fresh candy colours, offers a delightful shopping experience. On the open-plan ground floor, there is a state-of-the-art kitchen where visitors can watch demonstrations and try out the newest gadgets. The aisles are spacious and products easy to find. A visit wouldn't be complete without trying out Steven and Maj Doherty's dishes in the first-floor café. Steven was the first British chef to head a three-Michelin-Star establishment.

Lakeland's motto could be the founder's guiding principle: 'We take care of our customers and the business takes care of itself.' The story began with the humble plastic bags that Alan Rayner used to wrap chickens in on market days. When home freezing became the next new thing, the company offered freezing and storing equipment. By then their mail order was very popular. The next step was a watershed in the firm's history, as Sam Rayner explains in their golden anniversary celebration book: 'In a moment of inspiration, we got a glimpse of what must seem blindingly obvious to anyone now: people who froze food also cook it.' Soon the demand for cooking equipment outweighed everything else.

The operations are now a far cry from the days when the Rayner brothers used to wheel parcels to the local post office on a trolley for pocket money but, in the words of Wendy Miranda, Lakeland's Customer Ambassador, 'Some things have never altered such as the warm family feeling and the brothers' genuine care for their staff and customers.'

Address Alexandra Buildings, Windermere, LA23 1BQ, +44 (0)1539 488100, www.lakeland.co.uk | **Getting there** Next to Windermere railway and coach station. By car, approach Windermere on A591 and follow the signs for the railway station; free parking on site. | **Hours** Mon–Fri 8am–7pm, Sat 9am–6pm, Sun 11am–5pm | **Tip** Next to Lakeland is another retailing success story in the north of England: Booths. The chain focuses on regional produce with specialist fish, meat and deli departments.

110 _ Orrest Head

The walk that changed a young man's life

There is no lack of hills to climb in the area, but Orrest Head is special, owing to its association with Alfred Wainwright, the famous fell-walker. It was the very first hill the 23-year-old Wainwright climbed. He went on to inspire many others to walk in his footsteps. Years later, Wainwright wrote about this fell, 'Our first ascent in Lakeland, our first sight of mountains in tumultuous array, across glittering waters, our awakening to beauty.'

A clear day is a must to enjoy the breathtaking panorama of the central mountains. Directly and more prominently in front is the Coniston Old Man range. Further right are the Crinkle Crags with Pike O'Blisco in the foreground. The view extends to the Scafell range, with the Pikes of Langdale visible in the distance. Below you are the shores of Lake Windermere, its islands and bobbing sailboats. Wainwright was so enchanted by this panorama that the revelation changed his life. Eventually, he would set up home in Cumbria and spend his life exploring the fells.

Orrest Head is 210 metres above sea level, and is climbed directly from the edge of Windermere town. The start is clearly visible and it's a comfortable path, slightly rugged in places, leading all the way to the summit. There are resting stations here and there to enjoy more stunning views. At the summit, there is a large platform with an indicator pointing out the various landmarks, a plaque commemorating Wainwright's first summit and more benches. In theory, it's feasible to walk to the Head and back in under an hour, but it's much more pleasant to take a little more time to do the complete walk beyond the Head, across the fields and back through the woods of Elleray Bank.

The whole route is clearly indicated at the top but take a map along just in case you get distracted by the local flora and fauna. Try to spot the woodpeckers.

Address Windermere, LA23 1AP | Getting there There is a lot of parking in Windermere. The start of the walk is at the junction of A591 and A 5074, just opposite the entrance to Windermere station. | Access Year-round | Tip Gummer's How is another summit, on the eastern shore of Windermere, which suits all fitness levels and provides fantastic views of the area. It has an OS trig point at the top.

111__Lookout

Up for hours, down for minutes

Andy Plant makes mechanical sculptures, many of which are clocks, and all of which are objects of wonderment. His clocks are big, fun, extravagant. *Lookout* in Workington town centre is no exception. It was commissioned by the local council as part of a regeneration project involving a series of new public art and retail developments. *Lookout* was switched on by the Mayor of Allerdale in July 2006, and has since provided much more than just accurate time.

Plant's first proposal was a giant steel cone called *Nurturing Clock*, an animated garden nurtured by its host, the clock. *Lookout* has its roots in the area's long history of iron and steel making. Based on the design of the camera obscura, the clock's beam-like minute hand is essentially a long periscope intended to give people a view of the town and the surrounding countryside. The camera at the end of it rises up into the air on the hour, showing viewers the skyline of Workington, with the Lake District fells in the background, via viewing windows dotted around the body of the clock. Goggle through a porthole on the giant, hollow, spherical steel body of the clock to admire it all.

Every clock worthy of the name needs to strike the hour and so this one does, in its own special way. Matt Wand, who has collaborated with Plant on several projects, composed the chimes for *Lookout*, inspired by the voices of local people interviewed for the project, which were then set to music. The tune plays on the hour and the half hour. Speakers and lights are built into the surrounding benches to enhance the experience.

As you admire *Lookout*, it is easy to forget that the sculpture has been designed to give the time. For this you'll have to look both up and down. The hours are on a ring at the top of the sphere and the minutes can be found on an even bigger circle inset into the ground.

Address Opposite NatWest, just off Pow Street on Ivison Lane, CA14 3DY | Getting there
Workington is linked by A 596 from Maryport, by A 595 from Whitehaven, by A 66 from
Penrith; good bus connections and the Cumbrian Coast; railway line connects Workington
to Carlisle | Access Year-round | Tip The Helena Thompson collection offers a rare
opportunity to see a 'luck'. The Luck of Workington Hall is a small agate cup presented by
Mary, Queen of Scots to Sir Henry Curwen. Should it be lost, good fortune will desert the
'House of Curwen' (www.helenathompson.org.uk).

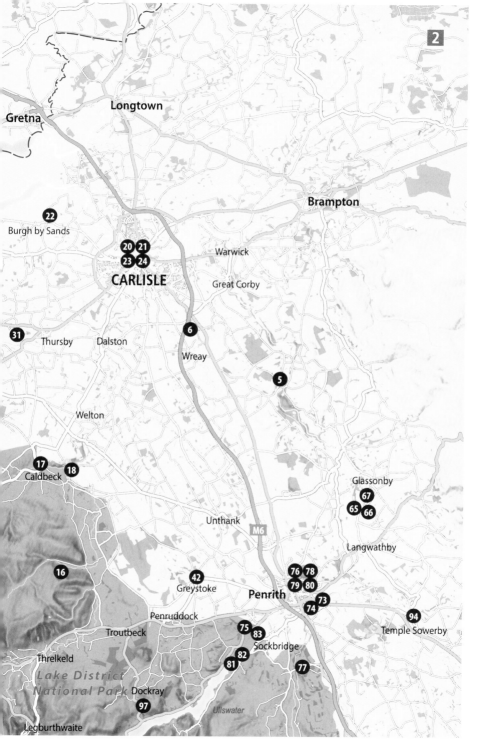

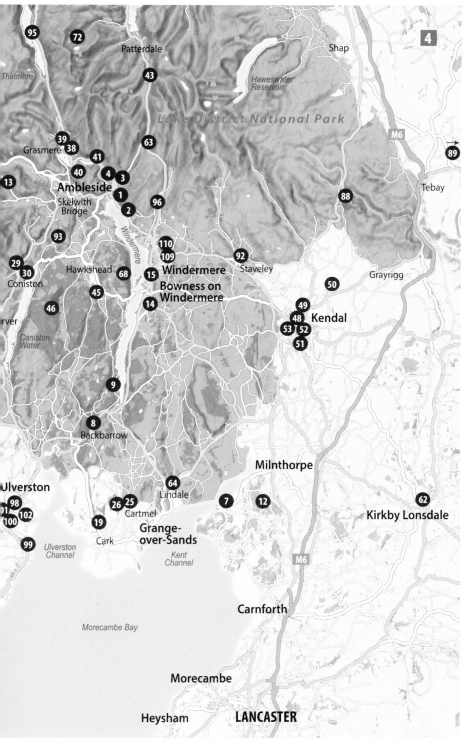

John Sykes, Birgit Weber
**111 Places in London
That You Shouldn't Miss**
ISBN 978-3-7408-2379-5

Solange Berchemin,
Martin Dunford, Karin Tearle
**111 Places in Greenwich
That You Shouldn't Miss**
ISBN 978-3-7408-1107-5

Ed Glinert, Marc Zakian
**111 Places in London's East
End That You Shouldn't Miss**
ISBN 978-3-7408-0752-8

Nicola Perry, Daniel Reiter
**33 Walks in London
That You Shouldn't Miss**
ISBN 978-3-7408-1955-2

Kirstin von Glasow
**111 Gardens in London
That You Shouldn't Miss**
ISBN 978-3-7408-0143-4

Laura Richards, Jamie Newson
**111 London Pubs and Bars
That You Shouldn't Miss**
ISBN 978-3-7408-0893-8

Emma Rose Barber,
Benedict Flett
**111 Churches in London
That You Shouldn't Miss**
ISBN 978-3-7408-0901-0

Ed Glinert, David Taylor
**111 Places in Yorkshire
That You Shouldn't Miss**
ISBN 978-3-7408-1167-9

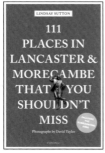

Lindsay Sutton, David Taylor
**111 Places in Lancaster
That You Shouldn't Miss**
ISBN 978-3-7408-1557-8

Cath Muldowney
111 Places in Bradford
That You Shouldn't Miss
ISBN 978-3-7408-1427-4

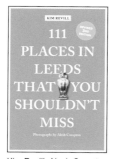

Kim Revill, Alesh Compton
111 Places in Leeds
That You Shouldn't Miss
ISBN 978-3-7408-2059-6

Michael Glover,
Richard Anderson
111 Places in Sheffield
That You Shouldn't Miss
ISBN 978-3-7408-2348-1

Julian Treuherz,
Peter de Figueiredo
111 Places in Manchester
That You Shouldn't Miss
ISBN 978-3-7408-2246-0

Julian Treuherz,
Peter de Figueiredo
111 Places in Liverpool
That You Shouldn't Miss
ISBN 978-3-7408-1607-0

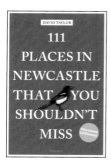

David Taylor
111 Places in Newcastle
That You Shouldn't Miss
ISBN 978-3-7408-1043-6

Katherine Bebo, Oliver Smith
111 Places in Poole
That You Shouldn't Miss
ISBN 978-3-7408-0598-2

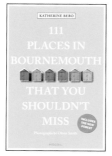

Katherine Bebo, Oliver Smith
111 Places in Bournemouth
That You Shouldn't Miss
ISBN 978-3-7408- 1166-2

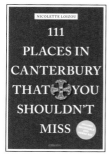

Nicolette Loizou
111 Places in Canterbury
That You Shouldn't Miss
ISBN 978-3-7408-0899-0

Philip R. Stone
111 Dark Places in England
That You Shouldn't Miss
ISBN 978-3-7408-0900-3

Rob Ganley, Ian Williams
111 Places in Coventry
That You Shouldn't Miss
ISBN 978-3-7408-1044-3

Martin Booth, Barbara Evripidou
111 Places in Bristol
That You Shouldn't Miss
ISBN 978-3-7408-2001-5

Alexandra Loske
111 Places in Brighton
and Lewes
That You Shouldn't Miss
ISBN 978-3-7408-1727-5

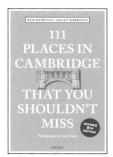

Rosalind Horton,
Sally Simmons, Guy Snape
111 Places in Cambridge
That You Shouldn't Miss
ISBN 978-3-7408-2376-4

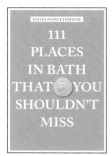

Justin Postlethwaite
111 Places in Bath
That You Shouldn't Miss
ISBN 978-3-7408-0146-5

Gillian Tait
111 Places in Edinburgh
That You Shouldn't Miss
ISBN 978-3-7408-1476-2

Tom Shields, Gillian Tait
111 Places in Glasgow
That You Shouldn't Miss
ISBN 978-3-7408-2237-8

Gillian Tait
111 Places in Fife
That You Shouldn't Miss
ISBN 978-3-7408-1740-4

Kai Oidtmann
111 Places in Iceland
That You Shouldn't Miss
ISBN 978-3-7408-0030-7

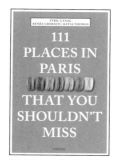

Sybil Canac, Renée Grimaud,
Katia Thomas
111 Places in Paris
That You Shouldn't Miss
ISBN 978-3-7408-0159-5

Thomas Fuchs
111 Places in Amsterdam
That You Shouldn't Miss
ISBN 978-3-7408-0023-9

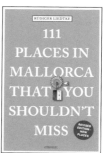

Rüdiger Liedtke
111 Places in Mallorca
That You Shouldn't Miss
ISBN : 978-3-7408-1049-8

Alexia Amvrazi,
Diana Farr Louis, Diane Shugart,
Yannis Varouhakis
111 Places in Athens
That You Shouldn't Miss
ISBN 978-3-7408-0377-3

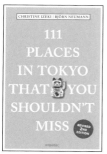

Christine Izeki, Björn Neumann
111 Places in Tokyo
That You Shouldn't Miss
ISBN 978-3-7408-1277-5

Jo-Anne Elikann
111 Places in New York
That You Must Not Miss
ISBN 978-3-7408-2400-6

Andréa Seiger, John Dean
111 Places in Washington
That You Must Not Miss
ISBN 978-3-7408-2399-3

Kim Windyka,
Heather Kapplow, Alyssa Wood
111 Places in Boston
That You Must Not Miss
ISBN 978-3-7408-2056-5

Acknowledgements

It's impossible to write a book like this alone, and I could not have done it without the following people: Simon for his invaluable support, Claire for her warmth and marmalade, Alison who worked tirelessly editing this book, every single person who showed me around, gifted me their time. You are too many for me to name each one, but you know who you are. Thank you so much.

Solange Berchemin was 18 when she travelled solo to the other side of the world, four years later, her partner took her to visit the Lake District. It was love at first sight. She has always enjoyed words and has a passion for people's stories. If there is a story somewhere she will find it. Ten years ago, after an atypical career path which led her to pick cotton in Greece and manage the largest languages department in London (not at the same time), she turned to writing. Columnist for the *Greenwich Visitor*, her articles have appeared in national and international publications such as *The Toronto Star*, *BBC Good Food*, *The Sunday Times*. She writes a blog and is the author of five books but when it gets too much she returns to the Lakes to collect more stories. To read her complete biography go to www.solangeberchemin.com.

The information in this book was accurate at the time of publication, but it can change at any time. Please confirm the details for the places you're planning to visit before you head out on your adventures.